THE JUDAISM BEHIND THE TEXTS

SOUTH FLORIDA STUDIES IN THE HISTORY OF JUDAISM

Edited by
Jacob Neusner
William Scott Green, James Strange
Darrell J. Fasching, Sara Mandell

Number 100
THE JUDAISM BEHIND THE TEXTS
The Generative Premises of Rabbinic Literature
IV.
The Latest Midrash Compilations:
Song of Songs Rabbah, Ruth Rabbah,
Esther Rabbah I, and Lamentations Rabbati and
The Fathers According to Rabbi Nathan
by
Jacob Neusner

THE JUDAISM BEHIND THE TEXTS

The Generative Premises of
Rabbinic Literature

IV.

The Later Midrash Compilations:
Song of Songs Rabbah, Ruth Rabbah,
Esther Rabbah I, and Lamentations Rabbati and
The Fathers According to Rabbi Nathan

by

Jacob Neusner

Scholars Press
Atlanta, Georgia

THE JUDAISM BEHIND THE TEXTS
The Generative Premises of Rabbinic Literature
IV.
The Later Midrash Compilations:
Songs of Songs Rabbah, Ruth Rabbah,
Esther Rabbah I, and Lamentations Rabbati and
The Fathers According to Rabbi Nathan

©1994
University of South Florida

Publication of this book was made possible by a grant from the Tisch Family Foundation, New York City. The University of South Florida acknowledges with thanks this important support for its scholarly projects.

Library of Congress Cataloging in Publication Data
Neusner, Jacob, 1932-
    The Judaism behind the texts : the generative premises of rabbinic
literature. IV, The latest midrash compilations: Song of Songs
Rabbah, Ruth Rabbah, Esther Rabbah I, and Lamentations Rabbati and
the Fathers according to Rabbi Nathan / by Jacob Neusner.
        p.   cm. — (South Florida studies in the history of Judaism ;
no. 100)
    Includes index.
    ISBN 1-55540-948-2
    1. Midrash—History and criticism. 2. Midrash—Sources.
3. Judaism—Essence, genius, nature. I. Title. II. Series.
BM514.N474 1994
296.1'4—dc20   93-48299
                                                     CIP

Printed in the United States of America
on acid-free paper

Table of Contents

Part Two
RUTH RABBAH

Part Three
ESTHER RABBAH I

Part Four
LAMENTATIONS RABBATI

Part Five
THE FATHERS ACCORDING TO RABBI NATHAN

Preface

...One must press behind the contents of the Mishnah and attempt to discover what the contents of the Mishnah presuppose....
E.P. Sanders[1]

Carrying forward Volumes I and II, in Volumes III and IV we move into two volumes of examination of Midrash compilations. The results of examination of Midrash writings, concluding here, shift in character, but their implications remain uniform, as I shall explain in the Introduction. Sanders's correct insistence that we "press behind" the contents of the documents – had he an interest in Judaism, he of course would not limit matters to the Mishnah! – yields a result no one could have anticipated, one that is only now emerging. In time I shall spell out the results of answering what is now proving to be not a wrong question, but a wrong-headed one.

It suffices here to explain that this protracted exercise asks a deceptively simple question of theory, applied systematically to the principal documents of Rabbinic Judaism in its formative age. It is, if I know this, what else do I know? If an author or compiler of a Judaic text tells me something, what else does he thereby tell me about what he is thinking or how? Can I press behind the contents of a Rabbinic document and attempt to discover what the contents presuppose? Can I ask about the author's premises: what he knows and how he thinks he knows it? Can I move back from the text to the intellectual context the text presupposes? The only way to find the answers to these questions is to reread documents, line by line, and see what lies behind what is there. This I do in a multi-volume exercise on selected, critical documents of Rabbinic Judaism. I now proceed to the second set of Midrash compilations, organized around books of Scripture, the ones produced

---

[1]E.P. Sanders, "Puzzling Out Rabbinism," in William Scott Green, ed., *Approaches to Ancient Judaism*. II (Chicago, 1980: Scholars Press for Brown Judaic Studies), p. 73.

(according to conventional opinion) in association with the Talmud of the Land of Israel, in the fifth century C.E.

All these writings, like the two Talmuds, are exegetical composites, and, it goes without saying, identifying premises and presuppositions in documents that are built as amplifications and clarifications of prior writings is not so simple. We have to eliminate from consideration what these documents have learned from the ones on which they depend, since what is secondary and derivative tells us not premises of later authors but lessons imparted by earlier ones. Hence our interest lies in what is fresh to the compilations under study: What do these writers bring to their work? That question forms the complement to the one we addressed to the Mishnah and the earliest Midrash compilations in sequence: What do these writers know before they start their work? In the case of the writings at hand, of course, what they know at the outset is Scripture; then what they think they know about Scripture forms the center of interest.

The goal of this project has now clarified itself. What I want ultimately to find out is whether I can identify premises that circulate among all or at least most of the Rabbinic compilations of Mishnah and Scripture exegesis. In the case of this Judaism, with its sizable canon of authoritative and holy books – Scripture, the Mishnah, Tosefta, two Talmuds, score of Midrash compilations – we want to know how the various writings hold together. Can we identify a set of premises that animate all writers, presuppositions that guide every compilation's compositions' authors and compositors' framers? If we can, then we shall have found what makes that Judaism into a single coherent religious system. If we cannot, then we shall have to ask a fresh set of descriptive questions concerning the theology of that religious system – a different set from those that guide the present work. When at the end of this exercise I reach the conclusion, in *Judaism from before 70 to 600: The Judaism That is Taken for Granted,* I shall exploit the facts that will turn up in the present book and its companions: Is there a Judaism behind the texts at all? And if not, what explains the coherence of the Judaism of the Dual Torah – for, by all reckoning, it is a remarkably cogent and stable religious system, with a body of ideas that for centuries have formed a single statement and today, with numerous variations and nuances, continues to say some one thing in many ways. Let me state with heavy emphasis what I want to find out:

At stake is not only the Mishnah and its premises (presumably bringing us back into circles of first-century thinkers) but the presuppositions of numerous representative documents of Rabbinic Judaism throughout its formative period.

The second question vastly outweighs the one that animates interest in premises and presuppositions: Is there a Judaism that infuses all texts and forms of each part of a coherent whole? At issue in the quest for presuppositions is not the Judaism that lies beyond the texts (which the texts by definition cannot tell us and indeed do not pretend to tell us), but the Judaism that holds together all of the texts and forms the substrate of conviction and conscience in each one.

That body of writings is continuous, formed as it is as commentaries on the Written Torah or the Mishnah, and the period in which they took shape for formal and substantive reasons also is continuous and of course not to be truncated at its very starting point, with the Mishnah, as Sanders's formulation proposes. For the Mishnah presents only the first among a long sequence of problems for analysis, and cutting that writing off from its continuators and successors, in both Midrash compilations and Talmuds, represents a gross error, one commonplace, to be sure, among Christian scholars of Judaism, for whom, as in Sanders's case, Judaism ends in the first century or early second and ceases beyond that point to require study at all. But the Judaism of the Dual Torah, viewed in its formative canon, is single and whole, and the premises and presuppositions of any of its writings, treated in isolation from those of all the others, contain nothing of interest for the analysis of that massive and complex Judaic system, only for the Judaism of a given piece of writing.

Let place into the context of contemporary debates the results presented here and in the companion volumes. An important premise of the sectarian study of the Jews and Judaism, besides the dogmas of a single, unitary, linear, and incremental Judaism and of the historicity of its sources, insists on the uniformity of all writings classified as canonical, that is, treated as the oral part of the Torah. The concept of a single, normative Judaism, on the one side, and of the facticity and historicity of all sources, on the other, explains why scholarship under parochial auspices ignored the lines of structure and order that marked the beginning of one document and the end of another. A theological premise, serving the religious institutions, drew attention to the status, as Torah, of all writings; if each document finds its undifferentiated place within the (oral part of the) Torah, then little effort will go toward differentiating one document from another. A historical premise concerning the contents of documents serves equally well to account for the problems not ordinarily addressed in the same setting. If, as we have seen, we take as fact all statements (except those concerning miracles) in all writings of the canon, then our inquiry concerns the facts documents supply; we shall take a position of indifference to the venue, origin, auspices, and authority, as to historical fact, of a given document and to relationships of documents to one another. All are held to draw indifferently upon a corpus of "tradition," deemed to have circulated orally hither and yon before coming to rest in a particular compilation.

Therefore, it was taken for granted, we open a document and come up with a fact, and which document yields what fact bears little meaning.

Not only so, but the paramount trait of all documents – their constant attribution of sayings to named authorities – afforded a distinct point of differentiation, namely, the names of authorities. Whatever is given to a specific name, whether in a document that reached closure ("only") two hundred years after he flourished or as long as five hundred or a thousand years later, serves equally well to tell us what said authority really thought and stated. Lives of Talmudic masters, along with histories of Talmudic times, therefore brought together, collected, and arranged in intelligible order, attributed sayings without a shred of interest in the time or place or circumstance of the documents that preserved them. The upshot, once more, was simple: considerations of time and circumstance do not register; every writing is equally useful; all may be assumed to wish to make the same, factual contribution to "the Torah," and, for the secular, history consists in opening a document, pointing to a sentence, paraphrasing the sense of that sentence, and speculating on its meaning: a labor of paraphrase and pure fabrication.

These theological and secular historical premises of course represented welcome labor-saving devices, since people took for granted it is not necessary to examine documents one by one, whole, complete, and in their own context. Not only so, but literary studies could take up a given trait or form, for example, the parable, and examine all evidences of the same without the slightest concern for comparing and contrasting the form of the phenomenon as diverse compilations portray it. And, still more common, scholars working on something we might call "the history of ideas" routinely set forth "the Talmudic view of...," collecting, arranging, and paraphrasing everything from everywhere, with little or no attention to questions of social context (not imagined to begin with to matter) or literary origin.

Entire careers devoted to expounding the Rabbinic, the Talmudic, or the Talmudic-Midrashic view of one thing after another yielded an entire library of monographs resting on the simple presuppositions now generally dismissed: [1] a single Judaism [2] revealed in a unitary tradition of completely reliable historical veracity [3] comes down to us in a variety of undifferentiated writings – a single book, with many chapters, not a library, made up of many free-standing, but cogently selected, volumes. The second appendix in this volume shows that I do not exaggerate the mindless character of the harmonistic approach to a complex set of books. That set of coherent premises explains why, moreover, people translated the documents in long columns of undifferentiated words, rendering impossible any sort of analytical work on the character, composition, and construction of documents, each viewed on its own, such as can be done if we identify chapter and verse, on the one side, or compose a still more serviceable reference system, on the other. The upshot was, the governing premises of the sectarian institutions dictated the character of the presentation of the sources in critical texts and translations and also predetermined the modes of characterization of their contents.

Today, by contrast, people understand that the documents viewed as free-standing and autonomous require description, analysis, and interpretation. Each exhibits its own differentiating traits. Not only do people grasp that the Mishnah is different from Leviticus Rabbah which is different from the Talmud of Babylonia. They also understand that each of those documents sets forth its own program in its own way. Systematic analyses of distinguishing traits of rhetoric, the logic of coherent discourse, and the topical programs of the various documents leave no ambiguity. Each writing exhibits its own formal traits, and each sets forth its own message. No document is readily confused with any other. Many, though not all, exhibit a cogency of program, working on the same few questions time and again. What that means for the received, sectarian episteme is simple. The point of origin of a given saying or story governs our reading and use of the item. True, some sayings and stories occur in more than a single document. The changes and developments of these items as they make their journey from here to there have to be traced, accounted for, if possible, in terms of the interests of the framers of the documents that make use of them. Among the parochial scholars, occurrence of the same sayings in the name of a single authority in two or more documents yielded "he often said." A different conception now prevails.

Scholars who take for granted that the Gospels yield not a single, harmonious life of Jesus but several distinct statements will hardly find surprising these simple rules of analysis. Each of the Rabbinic documents – the Mishnah, Tosefta, Midrash compilations, the two Talmuds – represents its own compilers, their taste and judgment in selecting from available compositions what they used and neglecting what they did not, their program in organizing and arranging and formulating matters in one way, rather than in some other. The collective statement and consensus of authorships (none is credibly assigned to a single author and all are preserved because they are deemed canonical and authoritative) show us how those authorships proposed to make a statement to their situation.

In fact, the question of a single, unitary, harmonious tradition, set forth in diverse compilations that themselves are not to be differentiated, is now settled. While most in the sectarian setting, and some in the academic one, may have yet to catch up to matters, the study of the

Rabbinic writings has drawn abreast of the study of the Gospels and other early Christian ones, and work on the characterization of documents, comparable to that on the Gospels, as well as on the differentiation of writings by appeal to their salient formal traits, is well advanced. As noted just now, documents are now perceived in three relationships: first, as autonomous writings; second, as writings connected with others of the same class; and, finally, as parts of a complete corpus deemed unitary and coherent: autonomy, connection, continuity beyond the key words to portray perspective. The labor is one of description, analysis, and interpretation, and it involves study of the text, its literary context, and its intellectual matrix.

DESCRIPTION OF THE TEXT AS AUTONOMOUS: a document is set on display in its own terms, examining the text in particular and in its full particularity and immediacy. The text will be described in accord with three distinct, differentiating traits: its rhetoric, logic, and topic: the formal traits of the writing, the principles of cogency that dictate how one sentence will link up with another, and the topical, and even propositional, program that the entire document addresses.

ANALYSIS OF THE TEXT IN ITS CONTEXT THROUGH COMPARISON AND CONTRAST WITH INTERSECTING AFFINES IN CONNECTION: a document connects with others in two ways, first and less important, through shared sayings or stories, but, second and far more important, through recurrent points of emphasis found in a number of documents. A set of documents may address a single prior writing, Scripture or the Mishnah; they may pursue a single exegetical program or take up a common question, deemed urgent in two or more compilations. They may intersect in other ways. Groups of documents may take shape out of an inductive examination of points of differentiation and aggregation.

INTERPRETATION OF THE MATRIX THAT BRINGS ALL CANONICAL TEXTS INTO A SINGLE CONTINUITY: the examination of the entire corpus of Rabbinic writings (or the writings found in the library at Qumran, or other groups of writings deemed by common consensus to form a textual community), finally, leads outward toward the matrix in which a variety of texts find their place. Here description moves from the world of intellectuals to the world they proposed to shape and create. That inquiry defines as its generative question how the social world formed by the texts as a whole proposes to define and respond to a powerful and urgent question, that is, I read the canonical writings as response to critical and urgent questions. A set of questions concerning the formation of the social order – its ethics, ethos, and ethnos – for example will turn out to produce a single set of answers from a variety of writings. If that is the case, then we may describe not only documentary cogency and the coherence of two or more writings but the matrix in an intellectual system that the continuity among many documents permits us to outline. That is the work that proceeds in the present part of the project.

The plan of the work as a whole is to examine important and representative writings – not every canonical document but only those that strike me as systemically generative, on the one side, or exemplary, on the other. My sense is that, if there really are premises of systemic consequence, they should turn up nearly everywhere, so that a sample of the documents must suffice. If that should not be the case, then the very notion of a single Judaism behind the Rabbinic texts will prove parlous, beyond all examination, testing, and demonstration, and probably untenable. But for now, I retain as my given the notion that the canonical writings of Rabbinic Judaism do come together and cohere, on which account a sample will suffice; others may pursue the same questions in the analysis of omitted documents. The following indicates how I plan to proceed with this project in particular:

IN PRINT

The Judaism behind the Texts. The Generative Premises of Rabbinic Literature. I. *The Mishnah.* A. *The Division of Agriculture* (Atlanta, 1993: Scholars Press for South Florida Studies in the History of Judaism).

The Judaism behind the Texts. The Generative Premises of Rabbinic Literature. I. *The Mishnah.* B. *The Divisions of Appointed Times, Women, and Damages (through Sanhedrin)* (Atlanta, 1993: Scholars Press for South Florida Studies in the History of Judaism).

The Judaism behind the Texts. The Generative Premises of Rabbinic Literature. I. *The Mishnah.* C. *The Divisions of Damages (from Makkot), Holy Things and Purities* (Atlanta, 1993: Scholars Press for South Florida Studies in the History of Judaism).

The Judaism behind the Texts. The Generative Premises of Rabbinic Literature. II. *The Tosefta, Tractate Abot, and the Earlier Midrash Compilations: Sifra, Sifré to Numbers, and Sifré to Deuteronomy* (Atlanta, 1993: Scholars Press for South Florida Studies in the History of Judaism).

The Judaism behind the Texts. The Generative Premises of Rabbinic Literature. III. *The Later Midrash Compilations: Genesis Rabbah, Leviticus Rabbah and Pesiqta deRab Kahana* (Atlanta, 1994: Scholars Press for South Florida Studies in the History of Judaism).

NEXT

The Judaism behind the Texts. The Generative Premises of Rabbinic Literature.
V. *The Talmuds of the Land of Israel and Babylonia* (Atlanta, 1994:
Scholars Press for South Florida Studies in the History of Judaism).

Judaism from before 70 to 600: The Judaism That is Taken for Granted.

I anticipate that the fifth of these *Vorstudien* will complete the
preparatory research and yield a clear account of what, indeed, is taken
for granted. That survey covering the main premises that are identified
in the documentary analysis will ask how the various premises and
presuppositions hold together: the intellectual foundations of the
Judaism of the canonical writings. That will present my first effort at
defining the unity of the Oral Torah, identifying the main principles that
transcend various documents but animate them all. The presuppositions
characteristic of the documents even now are proving, if not
contradictory, then at least, remarkably diffuse.

.   No work of mine can omit reference to the exceptionally favorable
circumstances in which I conduct my research as Distinguished Research
Professor in the Florida State University System at the University of
South Florida. I wrote this book as part of my labor of research
scholarship, expressed through both publication and teaching at the
University of South Florida, which has afforded me an ideal situation in
which to conduct a scholarly life. I express my thanks for not only the
advantage of a Distinguished Research Professorship in the Florida State
University System, which for a scholar must be the best job in the world,
but also of a substantial research expense fund, ample research time, and
some stimulating and cordial colleagues. In the prior chapters of my
career, I never knew a university that prized professors' scholarship and
publication and treated with respect those professors who actively and
methodically pursue research.

The University of South Florida, among all ten universities that
comprise the Florida State University System as a whole, exemplifies the
high standards of professionalism that prevail in publicly sponsored
higher education in the United States and provides the model that
privately sponsored universities would do well to emulate. Here there
are rules, achievement counts, and presidents, provosts, and deans honor
and respect the University's principal mission: scholarship, scholarship
alone – both in the classroom and in publication. Here at last I find
integrity, governing in the lives of people true to their vocation and their
mission.

I defined the work at hand in conversation with Professor William Scott Green, who gave me substantial help in clearly formulating my problem in its own terms. As ever, I acknowledge my real debt to him for his scholarly acumen and perspicacity.

JACOB NEUSNER

Distinguished Research Professor of Religious Studies
UNIVERSITY OF SOUTH FLORIDA
Tampa, FL 33620-5550 USA

Introduction

At stake in any study of a religion is the definition both of *that* religion and of *religion.* What I am trying to do here – after three full decades of continuous work – still is to find the correct way to define Judaism in its formative age. That is to say, to describe, analyze, and interpret the earliest stage in the formation of the Judaism of the Dual Torah. To that project, which has occupied me for thirty years, the question of premise and presupposition is critical. No one can imagine that the explicit statements of a generative text, such as the Mishnah or the Talmud of Babylonia, for example, exhaust all that that text conveys – or means to convey – about God's truth. With what Sanders correctly emphasizes in the statement at the head of the Preface no one can argue, and with that obvious premise, none ever has argued. To the contrary, even in the founding generation of the field that used to be called "Talmudic history," the true founder and greatest mind in the field ever, Y.I. Halevi, in his *Dorot harishonim* (Vienna-Berlin, 1923 et seq.), insisted that a statement rested on a prior history of thought, which can and should be investigated. He spelled out that premises of available facts yield a prehistory that we can describe. Everybody understands that the definitive documents of a religion expose something, but contain everything. Sanders is in good company.

But it is not enough to posit such premises; we have in detail to identify just what they were. So it is the task of learning to explore the premises, presuppositions, and processes of imagination and of critical thought, that yield in the end the statements that we find on the surface of the writings. But the work has to be done systematically and not episodically, in a thorough way and not through episode, anecdote, and example. We address an entire canon with the question: Precisely what are the premises demonstrably present throughout, the generative presuppositions not in general but in all their rich specificity? Here I take up this analytical problem, having completed my descriptive work.

The fourth and penultimate in a sustained project, this book therefore continues a protracted, systematic and detailed answer to two questions, first, the question set forth in Professor Sanders's quite reasonable proposal to "press behind the contents...to discover what the contents...presuppose." While Sanders speaks of the Mishnah, in fact the commanding question – if I know this, what else do I know about the intellect of the writers of a document or a whole canon? – pertains to the entirety of the oral part of the Torah. And the second question, as I have explained, is a still more urgent one: Are there premises and presuppositions that engage thought throughout the documents? Or are the documents discrete episodes in a sustained procession of thought that requires description upon some basis other than a documentary one?

The project thus presents an exercise in the further definition of the Judaism of the Dual Torah that encompasses not only what its principal documents make articulate but also what they mean to imply, on the one end, and how what they presuppose coheres (if it does), on the other. Since many of the answers to those questions are either obvious or trivial or beg the question, we have to refine matters with a further critical consideration. It is this: Among the presuppositions, the critical one is, which ones matter? And how can we account for the emergence of the system as a whole out of the presuppositions demonstrably present at the foundations of systemic documents? The program of this project, in three volumes for the Mishnah and further volumes for selected documents thereafter, aims at uncovering the foundations of the Judaism of the Dual Torah.

When I ask the general question about "the Judaism behind the texts," I refer to a variety of quite specific matters. All of them concern the premises or presuppositions of a document and of important statements within said document. I want to know what someone must take for granted as fact in order to make an allegation of some consequence within a legal or theological writing. Taking as our given what is alleged in a document, we ask, in order to take that position, what do I have to have known as fact? What must I have taken for granted as a principle? What set of issues or large-scale questions – fundamental issues that seem to me to pop up everywhere – has to have preoccupied me, so as to lead me to identify a given problem for solution, a given possibility awaiting testing?

These statements left unsaid but ubiquitously assumed may be of three kinds, from [1] the obvious, conventional, unsurprising, unexceptional, and onward to [2] the interesting, but routine and systemically inert, and finally to [3] the highly suggestive, provocative and systemically generative.

First, a statement in a text may presuppose a religious norm of belief or behavior (*halakhah* or *aggadah*, in the native categories). For one example, if a rule concerns itself with when the Shema is to be recited, the rule presupposes a prayer, the Shema – and so throughout. Such a presupposition clearly is to be acknowledged, but ordinarily, the fact that is taken for granted will not stand behind an exegetical initiative or intellectual problem to which a document pays substantial attention.

Second, a statement in a text may presuppose knowledge of a prior, authoritative text. For instance, rules in the Mishnah take for granted uncited texts of Scripture, nearly the whole of Tractate Yoma providing a particularly fine instance, since the very order and structure of that tractate prove incomprehensible without a verse-by-verse review of Leviticus Chapter Sixteen. Knowing that the framers of a document had access to a prior holy book by itself does not help us to understand what the framers of that document learned from the earlier one; they will have selected what they found relevant or important, ignoring what they found routine; we cannot simply assign to the later authorship complete acquiescence in all that a prior set of writers handed on, merely because the later authorship took cognizance of what the earlier one had to say. It is one thing to acknowledge, it is another to make use of, to respond to, a received truth.

Third, a concrete statement in a text may rest upon a prior conception of a more abstract character, much as applied mathematics rests upon theoretical mathematics, or technology upon principles of engineering and physics. And this set of premises and presuppositions does lead us deep into the foundations of thought of a given, important and systematic writing. In the main, what I want to know here concerns the active and generative premises of Rabbinic documents: the things the writers had to know in order to define the problems they wished to solve. I seek the key to the exegesis of the law that the framers of the Mishnah put forth, the exegesis of Scripture that they systematically provided. When we can say not only what they said but also what they took for granted, if we can explain their principles of organization and the bases for their identification of the problems they wished to solve, then, but only then, do we enter into that vast Judaic system and structure that their various writings put forth in bits and pieces and only adumbrated in its entirety.

Accordingly, this project, covering the principal documents of Rabbinic Judaism in its formative age, while paying attention to data of the first two classes, focuses upon the third category of presuppositions, stipulating that the first two require no more than routine inquiry. That is to say, we all know that the sages of the Rabbinic writings deemed the Scriptures of ancient Israel, which they knew as the written part of the

Torah, to be authoritative; they took for granted the facticity and authority of every line of that writing, to be sure picking and choosing, among available truths, those that required emphasis and even development. That simple fact permits us to take for granted, without laboring to prove the obvious, that the Judaism not articulated in the Rabbinic literature encompassed the way of life and worldview and conception of Israel that, in broad outlines, Scripture set forth. But that fact standing on its own is trivial. It allows for everything but the main thing: what characterized the specific, distinctive character of the Judaic system set forth in Rabbinic writings, and, it goes without saying, how the particular point of view of those writings dictated the ways in which Scripture's teachings and rules gained entry into, and a place for themselves in, the structure and system of the Judaism of the Dual Torah.

Prior to a vast number of rulings, generating the problems that require those rulings, a few fundamental conceptions or principles, never articulated, await identification. And, once identified, these several conceptions or principles demand a labor of composition: How does the generative problematic that precipitates the issues of one tractate, or forms the datum of that tractate's inquiry, fit together with the generative problematic of some other tractate and its sustained exegesis of the law? Once we know what stands behind the law, we have to ask, what holds together the several fundamental principles, all of them of enormous weight and vast capacity for specification in numerous detailed cases? Before we know how to define this Judaism, we have to show that a coherent metaphysics underpins the detailed physics, a cogent principle the concrete cases, a proportioned, balanced, harmonious statement the many, derivative and distinct cases of which the law and theology of Judaism are comprised.

What Rabbinic documents tell us that bears consequence for the definition of their Judaism in particular – not merely what was likely to be common to all Judaism, for example, a sacred calendar, a record of generations' encounter with God and the like – then requires specification, and the third of the three types of presuppositions or premises points toward the definition of what is at stake and under study here. That is, specifically, the deeper, implicit affirmations of documents: what they know that stands behind what they say, the metaphysics behind the physics (to resort to the metaphor just now introduced). For a close reading of both law and lore, *halakhah* and *aggadah*, yields a glimpse at a vast structure of implicit conceptions, those to which Sanders makes reference in his correct prescription of what is to be done: "...one must press behind the contents of the Mishnah and attempt to discover what the contents of the Mishnah presuppose."

Some of these implicit conceptions pertain to law, some to questions of philosophy and metaphysics, some to theology. Once we have examined important constitutive documents, we shall see that all of them circulate hither and yon through the law and the theology of the various documents; and only when we identify the various notions that are presupposed and implicit and show how they coalesce shall we understand the details of the Judaic system – law and theology alike – that comes to concrete expression in the Rabbinic writings. I have already set forth a systematic account, treating the Mishnah as a whole, of the document's premises in regard to philosophy, politics, and economics. These are large-scale exercises in answering the question, "if I know this, what else do I know?" My answer is, if I know the specific rulings of the Mishnah on topics relevant to economics and politics, I know that the Mishnah sets forth a philosophical politics and a philosophical economics. If I know how the Mishnah formulates and solves a problem, I know that the framers of the Mishnah thought philosophically – but mostly, though not entirely, about questions of a very different order from those that philosophers pursued.

This detailed work follows a simple and consistent program. Let me undertake to spell out the procedures of this and its companion volumes. What is needed is a patient sifting of details. Therefore I review the entire document under study here, and in each of its divisions and subdivisions examine data by the following criteria:

1. UNARTICULATED PREMISES. THE GIVENS OF CORRECT PUBLIC CONDUCT: I want to know what generative practices the halakhah at hand takes for granted, which customs or rites or social rules and laws are refined and improved, applied and analyzed, being simply givens. Very frequently, the law will provide detailed exegeses, in terms of a number of distinct cases and problems, of a single principle. The law therefore shows how in concrete and practical ways a principle operates. That is what is critical in this category.

2. UNARTICULATED PREMISES. THE GIVENS OF RELIGIOUS CONVICTION: At issue here are the givens of generative conviction: this category is identical to the foregoing, now with attention to matters within the native category of aggadah and the academic category of theology and exegesis. Where many texts presuppose the same premise but none articulates it, or the premise is never made explicit in such a way as to extend to a variety of cases, I classify the

matter as an unarticulated premise. But, I readily concede,
the difference between this category and the next is not
always obvious to me.

3.   MATTERS OF PHILOSOPHY, NATURAL SCIENCE AND
METAPHYSICS: This category covers general principles that
concern not theological but philosophical questions.
"Natural science" and "philosophy" for our documents
coincide, being two ways of referring to the same corpus of
knowledge. The questions that fall into the present category
are not theological but concern issues of natural philosophy,
science, and metaphysics, for example, sorting out matters of
doubt, discovering the rules of classification, working out
problems of applied logic and practical reason, and the like.
Now as a matter of fact, many rulings presuppose answers to
philosophical questions of a broad and abstract character.
Here we identify the premises of the documents that operate
widely but do not concern questions particular to the
situation of Israel.[1]

In *Judaism behind the Texts* Volume I.A, I asked also about two other
matters: points of stress and traits of self-differentiation. But these
produced nothing of sustained interest, only some casual and episodic
entries at which I thought a tractate or a major component of a tractate
struck me as laying heavy emphasis on a given proposition, on the one
side, or point of difference between the document's "Israel" and the rest
of the Jews, on the other. I found the categories too subjective for further
use, since I could not always identify the objective and indicative traits
that would lead me to categorize an item's premise as either a point of
stress or a point of differentiation. Accordingly, I omit these categories
from further use.

What I want to undertake in due course is a cogent account of all of
the premises that appear to me to play a role in the specific rulings of the
law, on the one side, and in the concrete propositions of theology and

---

[1]In some measure, also, I recapitulate the findings of *The Philosophical Mishnah.*
Volume I. *The Initial Probe* (Atlanta, 1989: Scholars Press for Brown Judaic
Studies); *The Philosophical Mishnah.* Volume II. *The Tractates' Agenda. From
Abodah Zarah to Moed Qatan* (Atlanta, 1989: Scholars Press for Brown Judaic
Studies); *The Philosophical Mishnah.* Volume III. *The Tractates' Agenda. From Nazir
to Zebahim* (Atlanta, 1989: Scholars Press for Brown Judaic Studies); *The
Philosophical Mishnah.* Volume IV. *The Repertoire* (Atlanta, 1989: Scholars Press for
Brown Judaic Studies). But the work done here is not focused so narrowly as the
survey accomplished in those volumes; I am more interested in finding as broad
a range of premises and presuppositions as I can. In *The Philosophical Mishnah*,
my program was carefully framed to identify clearly-philosophical matters.

exegesis, on the other. But that ultimate goal concerning the unity and coherence of the Judaism of these writings – the unity of the oral part of the Torah – is not going to be easily attained. Once we have assembled the data of all sixty-two tractates of the Mishnah (excluding Tractate Abot), we shall see how they relate to one another and even coalesce into a metaphysical structure and system.

It remains to explain that, when I refer to "generative premises," I mean to exclude a variety of other givens that strike me as demonstrably present but systemically inert. There are many facts our documents know and acknowledge but leave in the background; there are others, that is, premises and presuppositions, that generate numerous specific problems, indeed that turn out, upon close examination of the details of documents, to stand behind numerous concrete inquiries. The former are systemically inert, the latter, systemically provocative and formative. Such premises as the sanctity of Israel and the Land of Israel, the election of Israel, the authority of the Torah (however defined), and the like in these writings prove systemic givens, assumed but rarely made the focus of exegetical thought.

Not only so: a very long list of platitudes and banalities can readily be constructed and every item on the list shown to be present throughout the documents under study here; but those platitudes and banalities make no contribution to the shaping of our documents and the formulation of their system. Therefore, having proven that the sun rises in the east, from those systemically inert givens, we should know no more about matters than we did beforehand. True, to those in search of "Judaism," as distinct from the diverse Judaic systems to which our evidence attests, that finding – God is one, God gave the Torah, Israel is God's chosen people, and the like – bears enormous consequence. But that God is one in no way accounts for the system's specific qualities and concerns, any more than does the fact that the laws of gravity operate.

What makes a Judaic system important is what marks that system as entire and imparts to that system its integrity: what makes it different from other systems, what holds that system together. Defining that single, encompassing "Judaism" into which genus all species, all Judaisms, fit helps us understand nothing at all about the various Judaisms. But all we really have in hand are the artifacts of Judaisms. As the Prologue to Volume I.A has already argued, efforts to find that one Judaism that holds together all Judaisms yields suffocating banalities and useless platitudes: we do not understand anything in particular any better than we did before we had thought up such generalities. So by "generative premises," I mean, the premises that counted: those that provoked the framers of a document's ideas to do their work, that made urgent the questions they address, that imparted self-evidence to the answers they set forth. This brings us to the documents under study in this part of the work.

In the earliest Midrash compilations, not to mention the Tosefta, premises and presuppositions – "the Judaism behind the texts" – prove rare and episodic. The reason is that the character of the documents under study imposes limitations upon the free exercise of speculation. They undertake the systematic exposition of a prior document. Consequently, most of the task finds its definition in the statements that have been received and now require paraphrase, clarification, extension, and augmentation. The way in which this work is done – the hermeneutics that govern the exegesis of Scripture – yields no premises or presuppositions susceptible of generalization. And the result of the exegesis itself proves from our perspective sparse and anecdotal. Let me commence with a single example of how a sublime text is treated in a manner that, while not trivial, still in no way yields the kind of theological or moral or legal principles that at various points in the Mishnah show the document to rest upon deep foundations of thought. Our example is the exposition of the priestly benediction, and it shows us what to expect in the Midrash compilations that are treated here, therefore explaining, also, why the results of the survey prove frustrating:

XXXIX

I.1   A.   "The Lord said to Moses, Say to Aaron and his sons: Thus shall you bless the people of Israel. [You shall say to them: 'The Lord bless you and keep you, the Lord make his face to shine upon you and be gracious to you, the Lord lift up his countenance upon you and give you peace.' So shall they put my name upon the people of Israel, and I will bless them]" (Num. 6:22-27):

       B.   Since the deed required in the present passage is to be carried out by Aaron and his sons, the statement that is made is not only to Moses but also to Aaron and his sons.

       C.   For this is the encompassing rule:

       D.   Whenever the statement is made to the priests, then the deed is required only of the priests.

       E.   When the statement is made to Israel, then the entirety of what is required is incumbent on Israel.

       F.   When the statement is made to Israel but the deed is to be done by everyone, then one has to encompass proselytes as well.

II.1   A.   "The Lord said to Moses, Say to Aaron and his sons: Thus shall you bless the people of Israel:"

       B.   The blessing is to be said in the Holy Language [Hebrew].

       C.   For any passage in which reference is made to "responding" or "saying" or "thus," the statement is to be made in Hebrew.

III.1   A.   "The Lord said to Moses, Say to Aaron and his sons: Thus shall you bless the people of Israel:"

       B.   [This must be done when the priests are] standing.

C. You maintain that this must be done when the priests are standing.

D. But perhaps it may be done either standing or not standing?

E. Scripture states, "And these shall *stand* to bless the people" (Deut. 27:42).

F. The word "blessing" occurs here and the word "blessing" occurs there. Just as the word "blessing" when it occurs at the later passage involves the priests' standing, so here, too, the word blessing indicates that the priests must be standing.

G. R. Nathan says, "It is not necessary to invoke that analogy. For it is said, 'And the Levitical priests shall draw near, for the Lord has chosen them to serve him and to bestow a blessing in the name of the Lord' (Deut. 21:5). The act of bestowing a blessing is compared to the act of service. Just as service is performed only when standing, so bestowing a blessing is bestowed when standing."

IV.1 A. "The Lord said to Moses, Say to Aaron and his sons: Thus shall you bless the people of Israel:"

B. It must be done by raising the hands.

C. You say it must be done by raising the hands.

D. But perhaps it may be done either by raising the hands or not by raising the hands?

E. Scripture says, "And Aaron raised his hands toward the people and blessed them" (Lev. 9:22).

F. Just as Aaron bestowed the blessing by raising his hands, so his sons will bestow the blessing by raising their hands.

G. R. Jonathan says, "But may one then say that just as that passage occurs in the setting of a blessing bestowed at the new moon, on the occasion of a public offering, and through the medium only of the high priest, so here, too, the blessing may be bestowed only at the new moon, on the occasion of a public offering, and through the medium only of the high priest!

H. "Scripture states, 'For the Lord your God has chosen him above all your tribes' (Deut. 18:5). The Scripture compares his sons to him: just as he bestowed the blessing by raising his hands, so his sons will bestow the blessing by raising their hands."

V.1 A. "The Lord said to Moses, Say to Aaron and his sons: Thus shall you bless the people of Israel:"

B. It is to be done by expressing the fully spelled out Name of God.

C. You maintain that it is to be done by expressing the fully spelled out Name of God. But perhaps it may be done with a euphemism for the Name of God?

D. Scripture says, "So shall they put my name upon the people of Israel" (Num. 6:27).

V.2 A. "In the sanctuary it is to be done by expressing the fully spelled out Name of God. And in the provinces it is to be done by a euphemism," the words of R. Josiah.

B. R. Jonathan says, "Lo, Scripture states, 'In every place in which I shall cause my name to be remembered' (Ex. 20:20). This verse of Scripture is out of order, and how should it be read? 'In every place in which I appear before you, there should my Name be mentioned.' And where is it that I appear before you? It is in the chosen house [the Temple]. So you should mention my name [as fully spelled out] only in the chosen house.

C.   "On this basis sages have ruled: 'As to the fully spelled out Name of God, it is forbidden to express it in the provinces [but only in the sanctuary].'"

VI.1 A.   "The Lord said to Moses, Say to Aaron and his sons: Thus shall you bless the people of Israel:"

      B.   On this basis I know only that the blessing is directed to Israel.

      C.   How do I know that it is directed to women, proselytes, and bondsmen?

      D.   Scripture states, "...and I will bless *them*" (Num. 6:27), [encompassing not only Israel, but also women, proselytes, and bondsmen].

VI.2 A.   How do we know that a blessing is bestowed on the priests?

      B.   Scripture states, "...and I will bless them" (Num. 6:27).

VII.1 A.   "The Lord said to Moses, Say to Aaron and his sons: Thus shall you bless the people of Israel:"

      B.   It must be done face to face [with the priests facing the people and the people facing the priests].

      C.   You say that it must be done face to face [with the priests facing the people and the people facing the priests]. But may it be back to face?

      D.   Scripture says, "You shall say *to* them" (Num. 6:23), [which can only be face to face].

VIII.1 A.   "The Lord said to Moses, Say to Aaron and his sons: Thus shall you bless the people of Israel:"

      B.   The sense is that the entire congregation should hear what is said.

      C.   Or may it be that the priests say the blessing to themselves [and not in audible tones]?

      D.   Scripture says, "*Say* to them...," (Num. 6:23), meaning that the entire congregation should hear the blessing.

      E.   And how do we know that the leader of the prayers has to say to the priests, "Say..."?

      F.   Scripture says, "*You* shall say to them" (Num. 6:23).

Whatever the hermeneutics that is taken for granted, the unarticulated layer of law and theology is scarcely to be discerned; the givens are Scripture and its facts and formulations, on the one side, and a set of principles of exegesis deriving from a transparent hermeneutics, on the other. For our survey, I find nothing in the treatment of a passage of surpassing interest to enrich our grasp of the law or theology behind the text. What we see is what there is – that alone. When I observe that most of the documents surveyed here generate little of interest to an inquiry into the Judaism behind the texts, this passage speaks for me. What we derive is refinement and clarification, but the passage scarcely suggests that taken for granted is a deep layer of theological or moral speculation. What we see is what we get, which is, a text with some minor points of refinement.

Even though these results prove paltry, the issues remain vital, and a negative result itself bears formidable implications. Let me spell out what I conceive to be at stake in this protracted study. In fact, the issue of premises, the question, if I know this, what else do I know? – these form the entry point. But my goal is other. For the task of history of religions always is that of definition of religions: what we can possibly mean by those encompassing categories, "Judaism" or "Buddhism" or "Islam" or "Christianity" that descriptively conform to data. In the case of "Judaism," I want to know whether the construct refers to documents that cohere, or whether the fabricated category is imposed thereon. So I aim at finding out whether, and how, the various documents valued by the Judaism of the Dual Torah relate, not in imputed but in substantive ways. Do I find that the various writings that the Judaism of the Dual Torah produced in late antiquity rest upon shared and common fundamental convictions, that is, this "Judaism behind the texts," or does each piece of writing stand essentially on its own? It is clear that as a matter of theory documents that are held by those who deem them authoritative to cohere relate in three ways. First, they stand each on its own, that is, each is autonomous. Second, in some ways they may intersect, for example, citations or long quotations of one writing appear in some other. They are therefore connected in some specific ways. But, third, do these writings also form a continuous whole? That is what I want to find out in this exercise. Let me spell out these three dimensions of relationship, autonomy, connection, and continuity.

Documents – cogent compositions made up of a number of complete units of thought – by definition exist on their own. That is to say, by invoking as part of our definition the trait of cogency of individual units as well as of the entire composite, we complete a definition of what a document is and is not. A document is a cogent composite of cogent statements. But, also by definition, none of these statements is read all by itself. A document forms an artifact of a social culture, and that in diverse dimensions. Cogency depends on shared rhetoric, logic of intelligible discourse, topic and program – all of these traits of mind, of culture. Someone writes a document, someone buys it, an entire society sustains the labor of literature. But people value more than a single document, so we want to know how several documents may stand in connection with one another.

Each document therefore exists in both a textual and literary context, and also a social dimension of culture and even of politics. As to the former, documents may form a community whose limits are delineated by shared conventions of thought and expression. Those exhibiting distinctive, even definitive traits, fall within the community, those that do not, remain without. These direct the author to one mode of topic, logic, and rhetoric, and not to some other. So much for intrinsic traits. As to the extrinsic ones, readers bring to documents diverse instruments of intelligibility, knowledge of the grammar of not only language but also thought. That is why they can read one document and not some other. So one relationship derives from a literary culture, which forms the authorship of a document, and the other from a social culture. The literary bond links document to document, and the essentially social bond links reader to document – and also document (through the authorship, individual or collective) to reader. The one relationship is exhibited through intrinsic traits of language and style, logic, rhetoric, and topic, and the other through extrinsic traits of curiosity, acceptance and authority. While documents find their place in their own literary world and also in a larger social one, the two aspects have to remain distinct, the one textual, the other contextual.

It follows that relationships between and among documents also matter for two distinct reasons. The intrinsic relationships, which are formal, guide us to traits of intelligibility, teaching us through our encounter with one document how to read some other of its type or class. If we know how to read a document of one type, we may venture to read another of the same type, but not – without instruction – one of some other type altogether. The extrinsic relationships, which derive from context and are relative to community, direct us to how to understand a document as an artifact of culture and society. Traits not of documents but of doctrines affecting a broad range of documents come into play. The document, whatever its contents, therefore becomes an instrument of social culture, for example, theology and politics, a community's public policy. A community then expresses itself through its choice of documents, the community's canon forming a principal mode of such self-definition. So, as I said, through intrinsic traits a document places itself within a larger community of texts. Extrinsic traits, imputed to a document by not its authorship but its audience, select the document as canonical and make of the document a mode of social definition. The community through its mode of defining itself by its canonical choices forms a textual community – a community expressed through the books it reads and values.

So to summarize: the relationships among the documents produced by the sages of Judaism may take three forms: complete dependence, complete autonomy, intersection in diverse manner and measure. That second dimension provokes considerable debate and presents a remarkably unclear perspective. For while the dimensions of autonomy and continuity take the measure of acknowledged traits – books on their own, books standing in imputed, therefore socially verified, relationships – the matter of connection hardly enjoys the same clear definition. On the one side, intrinsic traits permit us to assess theories of connection. On the other, confusing theological and social judgments of continuities and literary and heuristic ones of connection, people present quite remarkable claims as to the relationships between and among documents, alleging, in fact, that the documents all have to be read as a single continuous document: the Torah. As we shall now see, some maintain that the connections between and among documents are such that each has to be read in the light of all others. So the documents assuredly do form a canon, and that is a position adopted not in some distant past or alien society but among contemporary participants to the cultural debate.

While I take up a community of texts and explore those intrinsic traits that link book to book, my inquiry rests on the premise that the books at issue derive from a textual community, one which, without reference to the intrinsic traits of the writings, deems the set of books as a group to constitute a canon. My question is simple but critical:

If in advance I did not know that the community of Judaism treats the writings before us (among others) as a canon, would the traits of the documents have told me that the writings at hand are related?

In this study, these "traits of documents" are the most profound and pervasive: premises and presuppositions. I cannot think of a more penetrating test of the proposition that the documents form a unity and are continuous with one another. The inquiry is inductive, concerns intrinsic traits of not form or proposition but premise, and therefore pursues at the deepest layers of intellect, conviction, attitude, and even emotion the matter of connection between document and document.

What makes the work plausible and necessary? It is a simple fact. All of the writings of Judaism in late antiquity copiously cite Scripture. Some of them serve (or are presented and organized) as commentaries on the former, others as amplifications of the latter. Since Judaism treats all of these writings as a single, seamless Torah, the one whole Torah revealed by God to Moses, our rabbi, at Mount Sinai, the received hermeneutic naturally does the same. All of the writings are read in light of all others, and words and phrases are treated as autonomous units of tradition, rather than as components of particular writings, for example, paragraphs – units of discourse – and books – composite units of sustained and cogent thought. The issue of connection therefore is legitimate to the data. But the issue of continuity is a still more profound and urgent one, and it is that issue that the present project is formulated to address.

With reference to the determinate canon of the Judaism of the Dual Torah, therefore, I ask about what is unstated and presupposed. I want to know the large-scale premises that form the foundations for the detailed statements of those writings. I turn to what is beneath the surface because I have completed my account of what lies right on the surface: the canon's articulated, explicit statements. It is time to look beneath the surface. In my tripartite program for the study of the Judaism of the Dual Torah in its formative age, an enterprise of systematic description, analysis, and interpretation, I have now completed the first stage and proceed to the second. Now that I know what the canonical writings say and have described the whole in the correct, historical manner and setting, I proceed to ask about what they do not say but take for granted. That defines the question here.

These questions bear a more profound implication than has been suggested. What I really want to find out here is not the answer to the question, if I know this, what else do I know? It is, rather, what are the things that all of the documents that make up the writings accorded the status of the Oral Torah know and share? When I ask about the Judaism behind the texts, I mean to find out what convictions unite diverse writings and form of them all a single statement, a cogent religious system. As I explain in the Introduction, every document stands on its own; each is autonomous. Many documents furthermore establish points of contact or intersection; they are connected. But, as a matter of fact, the Judaism of the Dual Torah maintains that every writing is continuous with all other writings, forming a whole, a statement of comprehensive integrity. If that is so, then at the premises or presuppositions of writings I ought to be able to identify what is continuous, from one writing to another, and what unites them all at their deepest layers of conviction, attitude, or sentiment. That is what is at stake in this study.

Accordingly, the experimental work of an analytical character that is undertaken here and in the companion volumes forms a natural next step, on the path from description through analysis to interpretation. From my beginning work on the Mishnah, in 1972, I have undertaken a sustained and systematic description of that Judaism. In 1992, twenty years later, that sustained and uninterrupted work reached its conclusion in the two volumes that state the final results of the two programs that I pursued simultaneously: description of the literature, description of the history of the religious ideas set forth in that literature. The results are now fully in print in a variety of books and have now been systematically summarized, for a broad academic audience, in my *Introduction to Rabbinic Literature* and *Rabbinic Judaism: A Historical Introduction* (New York, 1994 and 1995, respectively: Doubleday Anchor Reference Library). These two books state my final results for the description of the literature and the history of Rabbinic Judaism; at this time, I have nothing to add to the descriptive process, and not much to change in the results set forth over this long span of time.

In finding the way into the deeper layers of conviction and consciousness of the Rabbinic documents, I propose to move inward from my description of Rabbinic Judaism, its writings and its historical development, document by document, to the analysis of the inner structure of that Judaism; and this search, in due course, should open the way to an interpretation of the system of that same Judaism. Here I offer the first results of the analytical work, consequent upon completed description, that I have considered for some time. When these research reports have accomplished their purpose, I shall attempt to describe the Judaism behind the texts – if any.

It remains to note that Volumes III and IV of this work yield results of a limited, theological character. I find little of note for our survey of the premises and presuppositions of a legal character, and nothing of philosophical interest at all. To preserve the uniformity of the inquiry, I continue to introduce the rubrics for law and philosophy, even though theology alone proves of interest. In the following passage, out of Song of Songs Rabbah, our sages of blessed memory made the same observation as to the character of the writings under study here:

XXII

II.1   A.   It has been taught on Tannaite authority: when a person is not ill, he eats whatever he finds. When he gets sick, he wants to eat all sorts of sweets.

        B.   Said R. Isaac, "In the past, the Torah was worked out in encompassing principles, [Simon: the main outlines of the Torah were known to all], so people wanted to hear a teaching of the Mishnah or of the Talmud.

        C.   "Now that the Torah is not worked out in encompassing principles, [Simon: the main outlines of the Torah are not known] people want to hear a teaching of Scripture or a teaching of lore."

        D.   Said R. Levi, "In the past, when money was available, people wanted to hear a teaching of the Mishnah or law or Talmud.

        E.   "Now that money is scarce, so that people are sick on account of subjugation, people want to hear only words of blessing and consolation."

These words they found in the documents presented in Volume III and especially in the present one. Volume V will formulate in the context of the two Talmuds precisely the same issue as has governed here: Just what do our sages of blessed memory take for granted as premise of discourse, in specific contexts and also in general? Then comes the decisive question: Do the premises and presuppositions that emerge from various writings in the canon of Judaism join together to make a coherent statement, that is, do we find a single Judaism that forms the foundations of all of these documents in all their specificity?

Part One

SONG OF SONGS RABBAH

1

Song of Songs Rabbah Parashah One

I. The Character of Song of Songs Rabbah

Song of Songs (in the Christian Bible, "Song of Solomon") finds a place in the Torah because the collection of love songs in fact speaks about the relationship between God and Israel. The intent of the compilers of Song of Songs Rabbah is to justify that reading. What this means in fact is that Midrash exegesis turns to everyday experience – the love of husband and wife – for a metaphor for God's love for Israel and Israel's love for God. Then, when Solomon's song says, "O that you would kiss me with the kisses of your mouth! For your love is better than wine," (Song 1:2), sages of blessed memory think of how God kissed Israel. Reading the Song of Songs as a metaphor, the Judaic sages state in a systematic and orderly way their entire structure and system.

Our sages of blessed memory read the Song of Songs as a paean of praise for Israel, on account of Israel's love of God. This hermeneutic is stated explicitly and articulated throughout their reading of the document:

XXI

I.1   A.   "He brought me to the wine cellar, [and his banner over me was love]":

       B.   R. Meir and R. Judah:

       C.   R. Meir says, "Said the Congregation of Israel, 'The impulse to do evil took hold of me through wine, and I said to the calf, "These are your gods, Israel" (Ex. 32:4).

       D.   "'When wine gets into someone, it mixes up his mind.'"

       E.   Said to him R. Judah, "That's enough for you, Meir! People interpret the Song of Songs not in a derogatory way but only in a praiseworthy way [for Israel],

       F.   "for the Song of Songs was given only for Israel's praise.

       G.   "And what is the meaning of, 'He brought me to the wine cellar'?

H.   "Said the Congregation of Israel, 'The Holy One, blessed be He,
      "brought me" to the great wine cellar, meaning, to Sinai.

I.   "'["and his banner over me was love]": and he placed over me there
      banners of the Torah, religious duties, and good deeds.

J.   "'And with great love did I accept them.'"

With this governing hermeneutic in mind, we cannot find surprising that
the document proves repetitive, finding the same point in many
passages. Without recording each time a given point is made, we shall
accomplish our goal for this part of the analysis. That means the later
sections of this part of the work will appear somewhat cursory.

The repetitious quality of the compilation derives from the modes of
thought and expression that characterize it. To explain, we begin with a
simple equation. If the Talmud of Babylonia joined the Mishnah to
Scripture in its formation of the structure of the Dual Torah as one, so,
too, Song of Songs Rabbah joined metaphor to theology, symbol to
structure, in setting forth that same whole. Standing in the same period,
at the end of the canonical process, in the sixth century, its authorship
accomplished in its way that same summa that the authorship of the
Bavli set forth. But the writers and compilers worked with far more
delicate matters, those which deal with not intellect but sentiment, not
proposition but attitude and emotion. For the Bavli rules over the mind
and tells what to think and do, while Song of Songs Rabbah tells how to
think and feel.

Mishnah-tractate Yadayyim 3:5 defines the setting in which sages
took up the Song of Songs. The issue is, which documents are regarded
as holy, among the received canon of ancient Israel. The specific problem
focuses upon Qohelet ("Ecclesiastes") and the Song of Songs. The terms
of the issue derive from the matter of uncleanness. For our purpose, it
suffices to know that if a document is holy, then it is held to be unclean,
meaning, if one touches the document, he has to undergo a process of
purification before he can eat food in a certain status of sanctification (the
details are unimportant here) or, when the Temple stood, go to the
Temple. What that meant in practice is, people will be quite cautious
about handling such documents, which then will be regarded as subject
to special protection. So when sages declare that a parchment or hide on
which certain words are written imparts uncleanness to hands, they
mean to say, those words, and the object on which they are written, must
be handled reverently and thoughtfully.

All sacred scriptures impart uncleanness to hands. The Song of
Songs and Qohelet impart uncleanness to hands.

R. Judah says, "The Song of Songs imparts uncleanness to hands,
but as to Qohelet there is dispute."

R. Yosé says, "Qohelet does not impart uncleanness to hands, but as to Song of Songs there is dispute."

Rabbi Simeon says, "Qohelet is among the lenient rulings of the House of Shammai and strict rulings of the House of Hillel."

Said R. Simeon b. Azzai, "I have a tradition from the testimony of the seventy-two elders, on the day on which they seated R. Eleazar b. Azariah in the session, that the Song of Songs and Qohelet do impart uncleanness to hands."

Said R. Aqiba, "Heaven forbid! No Israelite man ever disputed concerning Song of Songs that it imparts uncleanness to hands. For the entire age is not so worthy as the day on which the Song of Songs was given to Israel. For all the scriptures are holy, but the Song of Songs is holiest of all. And if they disputed, they disputed only concerning Qohelet."

Said R. Yohanan b. Joshua the son of R. Aqiba's father-in-law, according to the words of Ben Azzai, "Indeed did they dispute, and indeed did they come to a decision."

Mishnah-tractate Yadayim 3:5

Clearly, the Mishnah passage, ca. 200, records a point at which the status of the Song of Songs is in doubt. By the time of the compilation of Song of Songs Rabbah, that question had been settled. Everybody took for granted that our document is holy for the reason given.

The sages who compiled Song of Songs Rabbah read the Song of Songs as a sequence of statements of urgent love between God and Israel, the holy people. How they convey the intensity of Israel's love of God forms the point of special interest in this document. For it is not in propositions that they choose to speak, but in the medium of symbols. Sages here use language as a repertoire of opaque symbols in the form of words. They set forth sequences of words that connote meanings, elicit emotions, stand for events, form the verbal equivalent of pictures or music or dance or poetry. Through the repertoire of these verbal symbols and their arrangement and rearrangement, the message the authors wish to convey emerges: not in so many words, but through words nonetheless. Sages chose for their compilation appeal to a highly restricted list of implicit meanings, calling upon some very few events or persons, repeatedly identifying these as the expressions of God's profound affection for Israel, and Israel's deep love for God. The message of the document comes not so much from stories of what happened or did not happen, assertions of truth or denials of error, but rather from the repetitious rehearsal of sets of symbols.

The character of discourse of the document, however, is such that we do not find theological (let alone philosophical or legal) propositions, therefore premises or presuppositions, in volume commensurate to the size of the compilation. The reason is that we deal here with other than propositional discourse, and to reduce the whole to the propositions that sustain the presentation is to endow the compilation with a character and an intention that do not pertain. Let me give a single example of why we may not expect rich returns for the present project:

II

VIII.1 A.　Another explanation of the verse, "For your love is better than wine":

B.　Words of the Torah are compared to water, wine, oil, honey, and milk.

VIII.2 A.　To water: "Ho, everyone who thirsts come for water" (Isa. 55:1).

B.　Just as water is from one end of the world to the other, "To him who spread forth the earth above the waters" (Ps. 136:6), so the Torah is from one end of the world to the other, "The measure thereof is longer than the earth" (Job 11:9).

C.　Just as water is life for the world, "A fountain of gardens, a well of living waters" (Song 4:15), so the Torah is life for the world, "For they are life to those who find them and health for all their flesh" (Prov. 4:22); "Come, buy and eat" (Isa. 55:1).

D.　Just as water is from heaven, "At the sound of his giving a multitude of waters in the heavens" (Jer. 10:13), so the Torah is from heaven, "I have talked with you from heaven" (Ex. 20:19).

E.　Just as water [when it rains] is with loud thunder, "The voice of the Lord is upon the water" (Ps. 29:3), so the Torah is with loud thunder, "And it came to pass on the third day, when it was morning, that there were thunderings and lightnings" (Ex. 19:16).

F.　Just as water restores the soul, "But God cleaves the hollow place which was in Levi and water came out, and when he had drunk, he revived" (Judg. 15:19), so the Torah [restores the soul], "The Torah of the Lord is perfect, restoring the soul" (Ps. 19:8).

G.　Just as water purifies a person from uncleanness, "And I will sprinkle clean water upon you, and you will be clean" (Ezek. 36:25), so the Torah cleans a person of uncleanness, "The words of the Lord are pure" (Ps. 12:7).

H.　Just as water cleans the body, "He shall bathe himself in water" (Lev. 17:15), so the Torah cleans the body, "Your word is purifying to the uttermost" (Ps. 119:140).

I.　Just as water covers over the nakedness of the sea, "As the waters cover the sea" (Isa. 11:9), so the Torah covers the nakedness of Israel, "Love covers all transgressions" (Prov. 10:12).

J.　Just as water comes down in drops but turns into rivers, so the Torah – a person learns two laws today, two tomorrow, until he becomes an overflowing river.

K.　Just as water, if one is not thirsty, has no sweetness in it, so the Torah, if one does not labor at it, has no sweetness in it.

L.　Just as water leaves the height and flows to a low place, so the Torah leaves one who is arrogant on account of [his knowledge of] it and cleaves to one who is humble on account of [his knowledge of] it.

M.　Just as water does not keep well in utensils of silver and gold but only in the most humble of utensils, so the Torah does not stay well except in the one who treats himself as a clay pot.

N.　Just as with water, a great man is not ashamed to say to an unimportant person, "Give me a drink of water," so as to words of Torah, the great man is not ashamed to say to an unimportant person, "Teach me a chapter," or "a verse," or even "a single letter."

O.　Just as with water, when one does not know how to swim in it, in the end he will be swallowed up, so words of Torah, if one does not know how to swim in them and to give instruction in accord with them, in the end he will be swallowed up.

P.　Said R. Hanina of Caesarea, "Just as water is drawn not only for gardens and orchards, but also for baths and privies, shall I say that that is so also for words of the Torah?

Q.　"Scripture says, 'For the ways of the Lord are right' (Hos. 14:10)."

R.　Said R. Hama b. Uqba, "Just as water makes plants grow, so words of the Torah make everyone who works in them sufficiently grow."

S.　Then [may one say,] just as water becomes rancid and smelly in a vessel, so words of the Torah are the same way? Scripture says that the Torah is like wine. Just as with wine, so long as it ages in the bottle, it improves, so words of the Torah, so long as they age in the body of a person, they improve in stature.

T.　Then [may one say,] just as water is not to be discerned in the body, so is the case with words of the Torah? Scripture says that the Torah is like wine. Just as with wine. its presence is discerned when it is in the body, so words of the Torah are discerned when they are in the body.

U.　[For] people hint and point with the finger, saying, "This is a disciple of a sage."

V.　Then [may one say,] just as water does not make one happy, so is the case with words of the Torah? Scripture says that the Torah is like wine. Just as wine "makes the heart of man glad" (Ps. 104:15), so words of the Torah make the heart happy, "The precepts of the Lord are right, rejoicing the heart" (Ps. 19:9).

W.　Then [may one say,] just as wine sometimes is bad for the head and the body, so is the case with words of the Torah? Scripture compares words of the Torah to oil. Just as oil is pleasing for the head and body, so words of the Torah are pleasing for the head and body: "Your word is a lamp to my feet" (Ps. 119:105).

X.　May one then say, just as oil is bitter to begin with, and sweet only at the end, so is it the case also with words of Torah? Scripture states, "Honey and milk" (Song 4:11). Just as they are sweet, so words of the Torah are sweet: "Sweeter than honey" (Ps. 19:11).

Y.　May one then say, just as honey has wax cells [that cannot be eaten], so words of the Torah are the same? Scripture says, "...milk" (Song 4:11). Just as milk is pure, so words of the Torah are pure: "Gold and glass cannot equal it" (Job 28:17).

Z.　May one then say, just as milk is [Simon:] insipid, so words of the Torah are the same? Scripture states, "Honey and milk" (Song 4:11). Just as honey and milk, when they are stirred together, do not do any harm to the body, so words of the Torah: "It shall be health to your navel" (Prov. 3:8); "For they are life to those who find them" (Prov. 4:22).

Now were I to reduce the foregoing to a proposition, it would obviously be, "The Torah is exceedingly valuable" or some such. And that platitude hardly requires articulation in the present setting. Hence we must take account at the outset of the simple fact that, while Song of Songs Rabbah rests upon an elaborate structure of beliefs of a theological character, specifying those beliefs not only does not do justice to the document, but it also does not vastly contribute to our research.

Rhetoric

The forms that govern the presentation of the document and of those that follow in this study are catalogued:

1. INTERSECTING VERSE/BASE VERSE FORM: the citation of a verse other than one in the document at hand (here: Song of Songs Rabbah) followed by a protracted exposition of that cited verse, leading in the end to a clarification of the base verse of the document at hand.

2. COMMENTARY FORM: citation of a verse clause by clause, with attached language, brief or protracted, amplifying that clause.

3. PROPOSITIONAL FORM: citation of a verse plus the statement of a proposition, proved by appeal to diverse verses, including the one originally cited.

4. PARABLE FORM: Parables very commonly begin with attributive language; they nearly always start with, "to what is the matter to be likened?" This may be explicit or implied, for example, simply, "to [the case of] a king who...." We are supposed to know that "to what may the matter be compared?" stands prior to the initial phrase. Then the author proceeds to set forth the parable. This need not take the form of a long story. It can be a set-piece tableau, for example, "the matter is comparable to the case of a noble family who had three representatives of her family at hand." The parable always follows a proposition, and the parable may then bear in its wake an explication of its components in terms of the case at hand, against as in the cited instance. And the parable may execute its purpose through a protracted narrative. So what makes a parable unique from

all other forms is not the narrative but the presence of an inaugural simile or metaphor.

5. THE DISPUTE: The dispute form here follows the model of that in the Talmud of the Land of Israel rather than the Mishnah. The formal requirements are [1] statement of a problem, for example, a word that will be explained, [2] two or more authorities' names, followed in sequence by [3] the repetition of each name and [4] a proposition assigned to that name. The explication of the propositional language may be substantial or brief, but the formal requirements of the dispute are always simple: names, then repetition of the names followed by fairly well balanced sentences, in which propositions held by two or more authorities on the same subject will be contrasted.

6. THE NARRATIVE IN THE FORM OF DIALOGUE: Here we have a protracted story, which unfolds through exchange of dialogue. The extrinsic narrative language is simply, "he said to him," "he said to him," and variations thereof. The entire tale is told by means of what is said. Verses of Scripture may or may not occur; they do not define a requirement of the form.

7. THE NARRATIVE EFFECTED THROUGH DESCRIBED ACTION, THAT IS, IN THE FORM OF A STORY OF WHAT PEOPLE DO: The story here depends upon described action, rather than cited speech. In this type of narrative we have a reference to what someone did, and the dialogue is not the principal medium for conveying the action. Rather, what the actors do, not only what they say, proves integral; details extrinsic to speech, for example, "now that man had a wife and two sons...," are critical to the unfolding of the tale. The explanation of what is done then forms the burden of the spoken components. The criterion for distinguishing narrative in the form of a dialogue from narrative in the form of described action is the burden placed upon the dialogue. If it explains action, then the action is the centerpiece; if it contains and conveys the action, then the dialogue is the centerpiece.

8. NO FORMAL PATTERN TO BE DISCERNED: A small number of items do not conform to familiar patterns at all.

Logic of Coherent Discourse

The document holds together its individual units of thought in a variety of ways. But the means for holding together those individual units in a large-scale composition is in one logic only, and that is, the logic of fixed association. So there is a mixed logic before us, one serving the compilers in their large-scale organization and composition of the whole document, the other serving the various authorships of the cogent units of sustained but completed discourse that are assembled by the ultimate compilers.

Topical Program

In reading the love songs of the Song of Songs as the story of the love affair of God and Israel, sages identify implicit meanings that are always few and invariably self-evident; no serious effort goes into demonstrating the fact that God speaks, or Israel speaks; the point of departure is the message and meaning the one or the other means to convey. To take one instance, time and again we shall be told that a certain expression of love in the poetry of the Song of Songs is God's speaking to Israel about [1] the Sea, [2] Sinai, and [3] the world to come; or [1] the first redemption, the one from Egypt; [2] the second redemption, the one from Babylonia; and [3] the third redemption, the one at the end of days. The repertoire of symbols covers Temple and schoolhouse, personal piety and public worship, and other matched pairs and sequences of coherent matters, all of them seen as embedded within the poetry. Here is Scripture's poetry read as metaphor, and the task of the reader is know that for which each image of the poem stands. So Israel's holy life is metaphorized through the poetry of love and beloved, Lover and Israel. Long lists of alternative meanings or interpretations end up saying just one thing, but in different ways. The implicit meanings prove very few indeed. When in Song of Songs Rabbah we have a sequence of items alleged to form a taxon, that is, a set of things that share a common taxic indicator, of course what we have is a list. The list presents diverse matters that all together share, and therefore also set forth, a single fact or rule or phenomenon. That is why we can list them, in all their distinctive character and specificity, on a common catalogue of "other things" that pertain all together to one thing.

What do the compilers say through their readings of the metaphor of – to take one interesting example – the nut tree for Israel? First, Israel prospers when it gives scarce resources for the study of the Torah or for carrying out religious duties; second, Israel sins but atones, and Torah is the medium of atonement; third, Israel is identified through carrying out its religious duties, for example, circumcision; fourth, Israel's leaders had best watch their step; fifth, Israel may be nothing now but will be in glory in the coming age; sixth, Israel has plenty of room for outsiders but cannot afford to lose a single member. What we have is a repertoire of fundamentals, dealing with Torah and Torah study, the moral life and atonement, Israel and its holy way of life, Israel and its coming salvation. A sustained survey of these composites shows the contradictory facts that the several composites are heterogeneous, but the components of the composites derive from a rather limited list, essentially scriptural events and personalities, on the one side, and virtues of the Torah's holy way of life, on the other. Here is a survey:

Joseph, righteous men, Moses, and Solomon;

patriarchs as against princes, offerings as against merit, and Israel as against the nations; those who love the king, proselytes, martyrs, penitents;

first, Israel at Sinai; then Israel's loss of God's presence on account of the golden calf; then God's favoring Israel by treating Israel not in accord with the requirements of justice but with mercy;

Dathan and Abiram, the spies, Jeroboam, Solomon's marriage to Pharaoh's daughter, Ahab, Jezebel, Zedekiah;

Israel is feminine, the enemy (Egypt) masculine, but God the father saves Israel the daughter;

Moses and Aaron, the Sanhedrin, the teachers of Scripture and Mishnah, the rabbis;

the disciples; the relationship among disciples, public recitation of teachings of the Torah in the right order; lections of the Torah;

the spoil at the Sea = the Exodus, the Torah, the Tabernacle, the ark;

the patriarchs, Abraham, Isaac, Jacob, then Israel in Egypt, Israel's atonement and God's forgiveness;

the Temple where God and Israel are joined, the Temple is God's resting place, the Temple is the source of Israel's fecundity;

Israel in Egypt, at the Sea, at Sinai, and subjugated by the gentile kingdoms, and how the redemption will come;

Rebecca, those who came forth from Egypt, Israel at Sinai, acts of loving kindness, the kingdoms who now rule Israel, the coming redemption;

fire above, fire below, meaning heavenly and altar fires; Torah in writing, Torah in memory; fire of Abraham, Moriah, bush, Elijah, Hananiah, Mishael, and Azariah;

the Ten Commandments, show fringes and phylacteries, recitation of the Shema and the Prayer, the tabernacle and the cloud of the Presence of God, and the mezuzah;

the timing of redemption, the moral condition of those to be redeemed, and the past religious misdeeds of those to be redeemed;

Israel at the sea, Sinai, the Ten Commandments; then the synagogues and schoolhouses; then the redeemer;

the Exodus, the conquest of the Land, the redemption and restoration of Israel to Zion after the destruction of the first Temple, and the final and ultimate salvation;

the Egyptians, Esau and his generals, and, finally, the four kingdoms;

Moses's redemption, the first, to the second redemption in the time of the Babylonians and Daniel;

the litter of Solomon: the priestly blessing, the priestly watches, the sanhedrin, and the Israelites coming out of Egypt;

Israel at the sea and forgiveness for sins effected through their passing through the sea; Israel at Sinai; the war with Midian; the crossing of the Jordan and entry into the Land; the house of the sanctuary; the priestly watches; the offerings in the Temple; the sanhedrin; the Day of Atonement;

God redeemed Israel without preparation; the nations of the world will be punished, after Israel is punished; the nations of the world will present Israel as gifts to the royal messiah, and here the base verse refers to Abraham, Isaac, Jacob, Sihon, Og, Canaanites;

the return to Zion in the time of Ezra, the Exodus from Egypt in the time of Moses;

the patriarchs and with Israel in Egypt, at the Sea, and then before Sinai;

Abraham, Jacob, Moses;

Isaac, Jacob, Esau, Jacob, Joseph, the brothers, Jonathan, David, Saul, man, wife, paramour;

Abraham in the fiery furnace and Shadrach Meshach and Abednego, the Exile in Babylonia, now with reference to the return to Zion.

These components form not a theological system, made up of well-joined propositions and harmonious positions, nor propositions that are demonstrated syllogistically through comparison and contrast. The point is just the opposite; it is to show that many different things really do belong on the same list. That yields not a proposition that the list syllogistically demonstrates. A single concrete example of how these lists work – and a brief one at that – is as follows:

XXIII

I.1 A. "O that his left hand were under my head":
     B. this refers to the first tablets.
     C. "...and that his right hand embraced me":
     D. this refers to the second tablets.
I.2 A. Another interpretation of the verse, "O that his left hand were under my head":

      B.   this refers to the show fringes.

      C.   "...and that his right hand embraced me":

      D.   this refers to the phylacteries.

I.3   A.   Another interpretation of the verse, "O that his left hand were under my head":

      B.   this refers to the recitation of the Shema.

      C.   "...and that his right hand embraced me":

      D.   this refers to the Prayer.

I.4   A.   Another interpretation of the verse, "O that his left hand were under my head":

      B.   this refers to the tabernacle.

      C.   "...and that his right hand embraced me":

      D.   this refers to the cloud of the Presence of God in the world to come: "The sun shall no longer be your light by day nor for brightness will the moon give light to you" (Isa. 60:19). Then what gives light to you? "The Lord shall be your everlasting light" (Isa. 60:20).

I.5   A.   Another interpretation of the verse, "O that his left hand were under my head":

      B.   this refers to the mezuzah.

What we see here is a repertoire of holy things – objects, events, persons can serve equally well and interchangeably – and if we simply state the theological point that the list is compiled to make, we scarcely do justice to the power and the art of the composition. This is how discourse takes place in the document; as noted earlier, the result is a very limited number of theological propositions and premises, expressed in an almost unlimited number of ways.

The list yields only itself, to be sure – but then the list invites our exegesis; the connections among these items require exegesis (of course, that is, eisegesis). What this adds up to, then, is not argument for proposition, hence comparison and contrast and rule making of a philosophical order, but rather a theological structure – comprising well-defined attitudes.

II. Unarticulated Premises: The Givens of Religious Conduct

1.   Studying the Torah is a way of entering the world to come:

I

V.1   A.   R. Phineas b. Yair commenced by citing this verse: "'If you seek it like silver [and search for it as for hidden treasures, then you will understand the fear of the Lord and find the knowledge of God]' (Prov. 2:4-5):

      B.   "If you seek words of the Torah like hidden treasures, the Holy One, blessed be He, will not withhold your reward.

      C.   "The matter may be compared to the case of a person, who, if he should lose a penny or a pin in his house, will light any number of candles, any number of wicks, until he finds them.

D.   "Now the matter yields an argument a fortiori:
E.   "If to find these, which are useful only in the here and now of this world, a person will light any number of candles, any number of wicks, until he finds them, as to words of Torah, which concern the life of the world to come as much as this world, do you not have to search for them like treasures?
F.   "Thus: 'If you seek it like silver [and search for it as for hidden treasures, then you will understand the fear of the Lord and find the knowledge of God]' (Prov. 2:4-5)."

Since what is at issue is behavior, it is appropriate to note the premise at hand, which is, proper actions lead the one who does them into the world to come.

III. Unarticulated Premises: The Givens of Religious Conviction

1.   Israel is the light of the world; Israel is the glory of the world:

III

III.1   A.   Another interpretation of the verse, "your name is oil poured out":
         B.   just as olive oil is bitter in the beginning but ends up sweet, so "though your beginning was small, yet your end shall greatly increase" (Job 8:7).
         C.   Just as oil is improved only by crushing in the press, so Israel accomplishes repentance only on account of suffering.
         D.   Just as oil does not mix with other liquids, so Israel does not mix with the nations of the world: "Neither shall you make marriages with them" (Deut. 7:3).
         E.   Just as oil poured into a full cup does not overflow with other liquids [not mixing with them, it overflows on its own], so words of Torah do not flow with trivial words.
         F.   Just as, with oil, if you have a full cup of oil in hand, and into it falls a drop of water, a drop of oil exudes on its account, so if a word of the Torah goes into the heart, correspondingly a word of trivial nonsense goes forth.
         G.   If a word of trivial nonsense goes into the heart, correspondingly a word of the Torah goes forth.
         H.   Just as oil brings light into the world, so Israel is the light of the world: "Nations shall walk at your light" (Isa. 60:3).
         I.   Just as oil is above all other liquids, so Israel is above all the nations: "And the Lord your God will set you on high" (Deut. 28:1).
         J.   Just as oil does not produce an echo [when poured], so Israel does not produce resonance in this world, but in the world to come: "And brought down you shall speak out of the ground" (Isa. 29:4).

XV

I.1   A.   "Behold, you are beautiful, my love; behold, you are beautiful; [your eyes are doves]":
       B.   "Behold you are beautiful" in religious deeds,
       C.   "Behold you are beautiful" in acts of grace,

D. "Behold you are beautiful" in carrying out religious obligations of commission,

E. "Behold you are beautiful" in carrying out religious obligations of omission,

F. "Behold you are beautiful" in carrying out the religious duties of the home, in separating priestly ration and tithes,

G. "Behold you are beautiful" in carrying out the religious duties of the field, gleanings, forgotten sheaves, the corner of the field, poor person's tithe, and declaring the field ownerless,

H. "Behold you are beautiful" in observing the taboo against mixed species,

I. "Behold you are beautiful" in providing a linen cloak with woolen show fringes.

J. "Behold you are beautiful" in [keeping the rules governing] planting,

K. "Behold you are beautiful" in keeping the taboo on uncircumcised produce,

L. "Behold you are beautiful" in keeping the laws on produce in the fourth year after the planting of an orchard,

M. "Behold you are beautiful" in circumcision,

N. "Behold you are beautiful" in trimming the wound,

O. "Behold you are beautiful" in reciting the Prayer,

P. "Behold you are beautiful" in reciting the Shema,

Q. "Behold you are beautiful" in putting a mezuzah on the doorpost of your house,

R. "Behold you are beautiful" in wearing phylacteries,

S. "Behold you are beautiful" in building the tabernacle for the Festival of Tabernacles,

T. "Behold you are beautiful" in taking the palm branch and etrog on the Festival of Tabernacles,

U. "Behold you are beautiful" in repentance,

V. "Behold you are beautiful" in good deeds,

W. "Behold you are beautiful" in this world,

X. "Behold you are beautiful" in the world to come.

2. The merit of Israel derives from the peoples' acceptance of the Torah at Sinai:

IV

IV.4 A. R. Yannai said, "The Torah had to be expounded only from the passage, 'This month shall be to you' (Ex. 12:2) [at which point the laws commence].

B. "And on what account did the Holy One, blessed be He, reveal to Israel what was on the first day and what was on the second, on to the sixth? It was by reason of the merit gained when they said, 'All that the Lord has spoken we shall do and we shall obey' (Ex. 24:7).

C. "Forthwith the rest was revealed to them."

IV.5 A. R. Berekhiah said, "It is written, 'And he told you his covenant [which he commanded you to perform, even the ten words]' (Deut. 4:13).

B.   "[Since the word for covenant and the word for creation contained the same letters, it is to be interpreted:] 'And he told you his book of Genesis, which is the beginning of the creation of the world.'

C.   "'which he commanded you to perform, even the ten words' (Deut. 4:13): this refers to the Ten Commandments.

D.   "Ten for Scripture, ten for Talmud."

IV.6   A.   And whence was Elihu son of Barachel the Buzite to come and reveal to the Israelites the innermost mysteries of Behemoth and Leviathan,

B.   and whence was Ezekiel to come and reveal to them the innermost secrets of the divine chariot?

C.   But that is in line with the following verse of Scripture: "The king has brought me into his chambers."

3.   Israel is like a woman now, but in the end of days will be like a man:

V

III.4   A.   R. Berekhiah in the name of R. Samuel b. R. Nahman said, "The Israelites are compared to a woman.

B.   "Just as an unmarried women receives a tenth part of the property of her father and takes her leave [for her husband's house when she gets married], so the Israelites inherited the land of the seven peoples, who form a tenth part of the seventy nations of the world.

C.   "And because the Israelites inherited in the status of a woman, they said a song in the feminine form of that word, as in the following: 'Then sang Moses and the children of Israel this song [given in the feminine form] unto the Lord' (Ex. 15:1).

D.   "But in the age to come they are destined to inherit like a man, who inherits all of the property of his father.

E.   "That is in line with this verse of Scripture: 'From the east side to the west side: Judah, one portion...Dan one, Asher one...' (Ezek. 48:7), and so throughout.

F.   "Then they will say a song in the masculine form of that word, as in the following: 'Sing to the Lord a new song' (Ps. 96:1).

G.   "The word 'song' is given not in its feminine form but in its masculine form."

III.5   A.   R. Berekiah and R. Joshua b. Levi: "Why are the Israelites compared to a woman?

B.   "Just as a woman takes up a burden and puts it down [that is, becomes pregnant and gives birth], takes up a burden and puts it down, then takes up a burden and puts it down and then takes up no further burden,

C.   "so the Israelites are subjugated and then redeemed, subjugated and then redeemed, but in the end are redeemed and will never again be subjugated.

D.   "In this world, since their anguish is like the anguish of a woman in childbirth, they say the song before him using the feminine form of the word for song,

E.   "but in the age to come, because their anguish will no longer be the anguish of a woman in childbirth, they will say their song using the masculine form of the word for song:

F.　　"'In that day this song [in the masculine form of the word] will be sung' (Isa. 26:1)."

IV. Matters of Philosophy, Natural Science and Metaphysics

Nothing pertinent to this category occurs.

2

Song of Songs Rabbah Parashah Two

I. Unarticulated Premises: The Givens of Religious Conduct

Nothing registers here.

II. Unarticulated Premises: The Givens of Religious Conviction

1. The history of Israel in Egypt, at the Sea, at Sinai, and subjugated by the gentile kingdoms, ends when the redemption will come. The entire message of history is contained within these theological statements:

XVIII

I.1   A.   "I am a rose of Sharon, [a lily of the valleys]":

         B.   Said the community of Israel, "I am the one, and I am beloved.

         C.   "I am the one whom the Holy One, blessed be He, loved more than the seventy nations."

I.2   A.   "I am a rose of Sharon":

         B.   "For I made for him a shade through Bezalel [the words for shade and Bezalel use the same consonants as the word for rose]: 'And Bezalel made the ark' (Ex. 38:1)."

I.3   A.   "...of Sharon":

         B.   "For I said before him a song [which word uses the same consonants as the word for Sharon] through Moses:

         C.   "'Then sang Moses and the children of Israel' (Ex. 15:1)."

I.4   A.   Another explanation of the phrase, "I am a rose of Sharon":

         B.   Said the community of Israel, "I am the one, and I am beloved.

         C.   "I am the one who was hidden in the shadow of Egypt, but in a brief moment the Holy One, blessed be He, brought me together to Raamses, and I [Simon:] blossomed forth in good deeds like a rose, and I said before him this song: 'You shall have a song as in the night when a feast is sanctified' (Isa. 30:29)."

I.5   A.   Another explanation of the phrase, "I am a rose of Sharon":

         B.   Said the community of Israel, "I am the one, and I am beloved.

C. "I am the one who was hidden in the shadow of the sea, but in a brief moment I [Simon:] blossomed forth in good deeds like a rose, and I pointed to him with the finger [Simon:] (opposite to me): 'This is my God and I will glorify him' (Ex. 15:2)."

I.6 A. Another explanation of the phrase, "I am a rose of Sharon":

B. Said the community of Israel, "I am the one, and I am beloved.

C. "I am the one who was hidden in the shadow of Mount Sinai, but in a brief moment I [Simon:] blossomed forth in good deeds like a lily in hand and in heart, and I said before him, 'All that the Lord has said we will do and obey' (Ex. 24:7)."

I.7 A. Another explanation of the phrase, "I am a rose of Sharon":

B. Said the community of Israel, "I am the one, and I am beloved.

C. "I am the one who was hidden and downtrodden in the shadow of the kingdoms. But tomorrow, when the Holy One, blessed be He, redeems me from the shadow of the kingdoms, I shall blossom forth like a lily and say before him a new song: 'Sing to the Lord a new song, for he has done marvelous things, his right hand and his holy arm have wrought salvation for him' (Ps. 98:1)."

I.8 A. R. Berekhiah said, "This verse ["I am a rose of Sharon, a lily of the valleys"] was said by the wilderness.

B. "Said the wilderness, 'I am the wilderness, and I am beloved.

C. "'For all the good things that are in the world are hidden in me: "I will plant in the wilderness a cedar, an acacia tree" (Isa. 41:19).

D. "'The Holy One, blessed be He, has put them in me so that they may be guarded in me. And when the Holy One, blessed be He, seeks them from me, I shall return to him unimpaired the bailment that he has left with me.

E. "'And I shall blossom in good deeds and say a song before him: "The wilderness and parched land shall be glad" (Isa. 35:1).'"

I.9 A. In the name of rabbis they have said, "This verse ['I am a rose of Sharon, a lily of the valleys'] was said by the land [of Israel].

B. "Said the land, 'I am the land, and I am beloved.

C. "'For all the dead of the world are hidden in me: "Your dead shall live, my dead bodies shall arise" (Isa. 26:19).

D. "'When the Holy One, blessed be He, will ask them from me, I shall restore them to him.

E. "'And I shall blossom in good deeds and say a song before him: "From the uttermost parts of the earth we have heard songs" (Isa. 24:16).'"

2. God saved the world only because of Israel:

XIX

I.5 A. R. Azariah in the name of R. Judah in the name of R. Simon [interpreted the cited verse to speak of Israel before Mount Sinai].

B. ["'a lily among brambles':] The matter may be compared to a king who had an orchard. He planted in it rows upon rows of figs, grapevines, and pomegranates. After a while the king went down to his vineyard and found it filled with thorns and brambles. He brought woodcutters and cut it down. But he found in the orchard a single red rose. He took it and smelled it and regained his serenity and said, 'This rose is worthy that the entire orchard be saved on its account.'

C.   "So, too, the entire world was created only on account of the Torah. For twenty-six generations the Holy One, blessed be He, looked down upon his world and saw it full of thorns and brambles, for example, the Generation of Enosh, the generation of the Flood, and the Sodomites.

D.   "He planned to render the world useless and to destroy it: 'The Lord sat enthroned at the flood' (Ps. 29:10).

E.   "But he found in the world a single red rose, Israel, that was destined to stand before Mount Sinai and to say before the Holy One, blessed be He, 'Whatever the Lord has said we shall do and we shall obey' (Ex. 24:7).

F.   "Said the Holy One, blessed be He, [Lev. R.:] 'Israel is worthy that the entire world be saved on its account.'" [Song: "for the sake of the Torah and those who study it...."]

3.   Israel's merit lies in its faith in God, expressed in accepting the Torah and carrying out its rules:

XX

I.1   A.   "As an apple tree among the trees of the wood":

B.   R. Huna and R. Aha in the name of R. Yosé b. Zimra, "Just as in the case of an apple tree, everybody avoids it in extreme heat, since it has no shade in which to sit,

C.   "so the nations of the world fled from sitting in the shade of the Holy One, blessed be He, on the day on which the Torah was given.

D.   "Might one suppose that the same was so of Israel?

E.   "Scripture states, 'With great delight I sat in his shadow,'

F.   "'I took delight in him and I sat.'

G.   "'I am the one who desired him, and not the nations of the world.'"

I.2   A.   R. Aha b. R. Zeira made two statements.

B.   "First: an apple produces blossoms before leaves,

C.   "so the Israelites in Egypt [Simon:] declared their faith before they heard the message:

D.   "'And the people believed, and they heard that the Lord had remembered' (Ex. 4:31)."

I.3   A.   R. Aha b. R. Zeira made a second statement:

B.   "Just as an apple produces blossoms before leaves,

C.   "so the Israelites at Mount Sinai undertook to do even before they had heard what they were supposed to do:

D.   "'We will do and we will hear' (Ex. 24:7)."

I.4   A.   R. Azariah made two statements:

B.   "Just as an apple completes the ripening of its fruit only in Sivan,

C.   "so the Israelites gave forth a good fragrance only in Sivan."

4.   God's presence takes place in Israel at the crucial turnings in the life of the people; God is present throughout; Israel is where God's presence takes place:

XXVI

I.1   A.   "My beloved is like a gazelle":

       B.   Said R. Isaac, "Said the Congregation of Israel before the Holy One, blessed be He, 'Lord of the world, you have said to us, [Simon:] "My love, my love." You are the one who says, "My love, my love" to us first.'" [Simon, p. 118: *Dew* is an exclamation of affection. Jastrow: Thou art sighing for us first, instead of our aspiring for Thee.]

I.2   A.   "My beloved is like a gazelle":

       B.   Just as a gazelle leaps from mountain to mountain, hill to hill, tree to tree, thicket to thicket, fence to fence,

       C.   so the Holy One, blessed be He, leapt from Egypt to the sea, from the sea to Sinai, from Sinai to the age to come.

       D.   In Egypt they saw him: "For I will go through the land of Egypt" (Ex. 12:12).

       E.   At the sea they saw him: "And Israel saw the great hand" (Ex. 14:31); "This is my God and I will glorify him" (Ex. 15:2).

       F.   At Sinai they saw him: "The Lord spoke with you face to face in the mountain" (Deut. 5:4); "The Lord comes from Sinai" (Deut. 33:2).

I.3   A.   "...or a young stag":

       B.   R. Yosé b. R. Hanina said, "Meaning, like young deer."

I.4   A.   "Behold, there he stands behind our wall":

       B.   behind our wall at Sinai: "For on the third day the Lord will come down" (Ex. 19:11).

I.5   A.   "...gazing in at the windows":

       B.   "And the Lord came down upon Mount Sinai, at the top of the mountain" (Ex. 19:11).

I.6   A.   "...looking through the lattice":

       B.   "And God spoke all these words" (Ex. 20:1).

I.7   A.   "My beloved speaks and says to me, ['Arise, my love, my fair one, and come away] (Song 2:10)'":

       B.   What did he say to me?

       C.   "I am the Lord your God" (Ex. 20:2).

III. Matters of Philosophy, Natural Science and Metaphysics

Nothing belongs under this rubric.

3

Song of Songs Rabbah Parashah Three

I. Unarticulated Premises: The Givens of Religious Conduct

There are no points of halakhah registered here.

II. Unarticulated Premises: The Givens of Religious Conviction

1. Israel's condition among the nations is brought about by neglect of the Torah and religious duties:

XXXV

I.2   A.   Said R. Levi, "Said the community of Israel before the Holy One, blessed be He, 'Lord of the world, in the past, you would give light for me between one night and the next night,

        B.   "'between the night of Egypt and the night of Babylonia, between the night of Babylonia and the night of Media, between the night of Media and the night of Greece, between the night of Greece and the night of Edom.

        C.   "'Now that I have fallen asleep [Simon:] neglectful of the Torah and the religious duties, one night flows into the next.'"

III. Matters of Philosophy, Natural Science and Metaphysics

Nothing pertains.

4

Song of Songs Rabbah Parashah Four

I. Unarticulated Premises: The Givens of Religious Conduct

While some halakhic paragraphs are quoted, the discussion does not take up their premises or build upon them.

II. Unarticulated Premises: The Givens of Religious Conviction

1. Israel's beauty in God's eyes lies in its fulfillment of the obligations of the Torah; covenantal nomism defines Israel's relationship to God:

XLV

I.1　A.　"Behold, you are beautiful, my love, behold you are beautiful":

　　B.　"Behold you are beautiful" in religious deeds,

　　C.　"Behold you are beautiful" in acts of grace,

　　D.　"Behold you are beautiful" in carrying out religious obligations of commission,

　　E.　"Behold you are beautiful" in carrying out religious obligations of omission,

　　F.　"Behold you are beautiful" in carrying out the religious duties of the home, in separating priestly ration and tithes,

　　G.　"Behold you are beautiful" in carrying out the religious duties of the field, gleanings, forgotten sheaves, the corner of the field, poor person's tithe, and declaring the field ownerless,

　　H.　"Behold you are beautiful" in observing the taboo against mixed species,

　　I.　"Behold you are beautiful" in providing a linen cloak with woolen show fringes,

　　J.　"Behold you are beautiful" in [keeping the rules governing] planting,

　　K.　"Behold you are beautiful" in keeping the taboo on uncircumcised produce,

　　L.　"Behold you are beautiful" in keeping the laws on produce in the fourth year after the planting of an orchard,

　　M.　"Behold you are beautiful" in circumcision,

39

N. "Behold you are beautiful" in trimming the wound,
O. "Behold you are beautiful" in reciting the Prayer,
P. "Behold you are beautiful" in reciting the Shema,
Q. "Behold you are beautiful" in putting a mezuzah on the doorpost of your house,
R. "Behold you are beautiful" in wearing phylacteries,
S. "Behold you are beautiful" in building the tabernacle for the Festival of Tabernacles,
T. "Behold you are beautiful" in taking the palm branch and etrog on the Festival of Tabernacles,
U. "Behold you are beautiful" in repentance,
V. "Behold you are beautiful" in good deeds,
W. "Behold you are beautiful" in this world,
X. "Behold you are beautiful" in the world to come.

2. God remembers the deeds of the patriarchs in the favor of their offspring through the generations:

I

I.1 A. "Until the day breathes":
B. R. Abbahu and R. Levi:
C. One said, "[Genesis Rabbah XLVII:VII.1. 'Then Abraham took Ishmael his son and all the slaves born in his house [or bought for his money, every male among the men of Abraham's house, and he circumcised the flesh of their foreskins that very day, as God had said to him]' (Gen. 17:23)]
D. "When Abraham circumcised himself, his sons, and those who were born of his house, he made a mountain of foreskins, and the sun shone on them, and they putrefied. The stench rose to heaven before the Holy One, blessed be He, like the scent of incense and like the scent of the handful of frankincense thrown onto the offerings made by fire.
E. "Said the Holy One, blessed be He, 'When my children will come into transgressions and bad deeds, I shall remember in their behalf that scent and will be filled with mercy for them and convert the attribute of justice into the attribute of mercy for them.'
F. "What verse of Scripture indicates it? 'I will hie me to the mountain of myrrh and the hill of frankincense.'"
G. R. Levi said, "When Joshua circumcised the children of Israel, he made a mountain of foreskins, and the sun shone on them, and they putrefied. The stench rose to heaven before the Holy One, blessed be He, like the scent of incense and like the scent of the handful of frankincense thrown onto the offerings made by fire.
H. "Said the Holy One, blessed be He, 'When my children will come into transgressions and bad deeds, I shall remember in their behalf that scent and will be filled with mercy for them and convert the attribute of justice into the attribute of mercy for them.'
I. "What verse of Scripture indicates it? 'I will hie me to the mountain of myrrh and the hill of frankincense.'"

III. Matters of Philosophy, Natural Science and Metaphysics

I find nothing that fits.

5

Song of Songs Rabbah Parashah Five

I. Unarticulated Premises: The Givens of Religious Conduct

I find nothing of halakhic interest.

II. Unarticulated Premises: The Givens of Religious Conviction

1. Israel failed in some ways, but succeeded in others, in serving God properly:

LXII

I.1   A.   "I slept, but my heart was awake":

       B.   Said the community of Israel before the Holy One, blessed be He, "Lord of the world, 'I slept': as to the religious duties,

       C.   "'but my heart was awake': as to acts of loving kindness.

       D.   "'I slept': as to acts of righteousness.

       E.   "'but my heart was awake': in doing them.

       F.   "'I slept': as to the offerings.

       G.   "'but my heart was awake': as to reciting the Shema and saying the Prayer.

       H.   "'I slept': as to the house of the sanctuary.

       I.   "'but my heart was awake': as to synagogues and study houses.

       J.   "'I slept': as to the end of days.

       K.   "'but my heart was awake': as to redemption.

       L.   "'I slept': as to redemption.

       M.   "'but [the] heart' of the Holy One, blessed be He, 'was awake' to redeem me."

2. God and Israel meet in history, at the Sea; and they meet in religious observances of holy time now, and finally, in the world to come:

LXX

I.1   A.   The Israelites answer them, "'My beloved is all radiant and ruddy."

       B.   "radiant": to me in the land of Egypt,

       C.   "and ruddy": to the Egyptians.

  D.   "radiant": in the land of Egypt, "For I will go through the land of Egypt" (Ex. 12:13).
  E.   "and ruddy": "And the Lord overthrew the Egyptians" (Ex. 14:27).
  F.   "radiant": at the Sea: "The children of Israel walked upon dry land in the midst of the sea" (Ex. 14:29).
  G.   "and ruddy": to the Egyptians at the Sea: "And the Lord overthrew the Egyptians in the midst of the sea" (Ex. 14:27).
  H.   "radiant": in the world to come.
  I.   "and ruddy": in this world.

I.2   A.   R. Levi b. R. Hayyata made three statements concerning the matter:
  B.   "'radiant': on the Sabbath.
  C.   "'and ruddy': on the other days of the week.
  D.   "'radiant': on the New Year.
  E.   "'and ruddy': on the other days of the year.
  F.   "'radiant': in this world.
  G.   "'and ruddy': in the world to come.

III. Matters of Philosophy, Natural Science and Metaphysics

Unsurprisingly, nothing qualifies for this rubric.

6

Song of Songs Rabbah Parashah Six

I find nothing not already recorded as a premise or presupposition in the present document.

7

Song of Songs Rabbah Parashah Seven

I identify nothing both fresh and relevant.

8

Song of Songs Rabbah Parashah Eight

I. Unarticulated Premises: The Givens of Religious Conduct

No halakhic matters enter into consideration.

II. Unarticulated Premises: The Givens of Religious Conviction

1. The Torah is what distinguishes Israel from the nations, and the Torah is the mark of God's love for Israel; the nations have no share in the Torah and no medium for achieving atonement:

CIX

I.1   A.   "Many waters":

           B.   This refers to the nations of the world: "Ah, the uproar of many peoples, that roar like the roaring of the seas" (Isa. 17:12).

           C.   "cannot quench love":

           D.   The love with which the Holy One, blessed be He, loves Israel: "I have loved you, says the Lord" (Mal. 1:2).

           E.   "neither can floods drown it":

           F.   This refers to the nations of the world: "In that day shall the Lord shave with a razor that is hired in the parts beyond the River...now therefore behold the Lord brings up upon them the waters of the River" (Isa. 7:20, 8:7).

I.2   A.   Another matter: "If a man offered for love all the wealth of his house":

           B.   If all of the nations of the world should open their treasuries and give their money in exchange for a single item of the Torah,

           C.   it would not achieve atonement in their behalf ever.

III. Matters of Philosophy, Natural Science and Metaphysics

The rubric remains useless.

Part Two

RUTH RABBAH

9

Ruth Rabbah Petihtaot

I. The Character of Ruth Rabbah

Like the other Midrash compilations of its class, Ruth Rabbah makes one paramount point through numerous exegetical details. Ruth Rabbah has only one message, expressed in a variety of components but single and cogent. It concerns the outsider who becomes the principal, the Messiah out of Moab, and this miracle is accomplished through mastery of the Torah. The main points of the document are these:

[1] Israel's fate depends upon its proper conduct toward its leaders.

[2] The leaders must not be arrogant.

[3] The admission of the outsider depends upon the rules of the Torah. These differentiate among outsiders. Those who know the rules are able to apply them accurately and mercifully.

[4] The proselyte is accepted because the Torah makes it possible to do so, and the condition of acceptance is complete and total submission to the Torah. Boaz taught Ruth the rules of the Torah, and she obeyed them carefully.

[5] Those proselytes who are accepted are respected by God and are completely equal to all other Israelites. Those who marry them are masters of the Torah, and their descendants are masters of the Torah, typified by David. Boaz in his day and David in his day were the same in this regard.

[6] What the proselyte therefore accomplishes is to take shelter under the wings of God's presence, and the proselyte who does so stands in the royal line of David, Solomon, and the

Messiah. Over and over again, we see, the point is made that Ruth the Moabitess, perceived by the ignorant as an outsider, enjoyed complete equality with all other Israelites, because she had accepted the yoke of the Torah, married a great sage, and produced the Messiah sage, David.

Scripture has provided everything but the main point: the Moabite Messiah. But sages impose upon the whole their distinctive message, which is the priority of the Torah, the extraordinary power of the Torah to join the opposites – Messiah, utter outsider – into a single figure, and to accomplish this union of opposites through a woman. The femininity of Ruth seems to me as critical to the whole as the Moabite origin: the two modes of the (from the Israelite perspective) abnormal, outsider as against Israelite, woman as against man, therefore are invoked, and both for the same purpose, to show how, through the Torah, all things become one. That is the message of the document, and, seen whole, the principal message, to which all other messages prove peripheral.

Through Scripture the sages accomplished their writings. It is not so much by writing fresh discourses as by compiling and arranging materials that the framers of the document accomplished that writing. It would be difficult to find a less promising mode of writing than merely collecting and arranging available compositions and turning them into a composite. But that in the aggregate is the predominant trait of this writing. That the compilers were equally interested in the exposition of the book of Ruth as in the execution of their paramount proposition through their compilation is clear. A large number of entries contain no more elaborate proposition than the exposition through paraphrase of the sense of a given clause or verse.

Indeed, Ruth Rabbah proves nearly as much a commentary in the narrowest sense – verse by verse amplification, paraphrase, exposition – as it is a compilation in the working definition of this inquiry of mine. What holds the document together and gives it, if not coherence, then at least flow and movement, after all, are the successive passages of (mere) exposition. All the more stunning, therefore, is the simple fact that, when all has been set forth and completed, there really is that simple message that the Torah (as exemplified by the sage) makes the outsider into an insider, the Moabite into an Israelite, the offspring of the outsider into the Messiah: all on the condition, the only condition, that the Torah govern. This is a document about one thing, and it makes a single statement, and that statement is coherent.

The authorship decided to compose a document concerning the book of Ruth in order to make a single point. Everything else was subordinated to that definitive intention. Once the work got underway, the task was one of not exposition so much as repetition, not unpacking and exploring a complex conception, but restating the point, on the one side, and eliciting or evoking the proper attitude that was congruent with that point, on the other. The decision, viewed after the fact, was to make one statement in an enormous number of ways. It is that the Torah dictates Israel's fate; if you want to know what that fate will be, study the Torah; and if you want to control that fate, follow the model of the sage Messiah. As usual, therefore, what we find is a recasting of the Deuteronomic prophetic theology.

Logic of Coherent Discourse

The logics work in the same way as those in Song of Songs Rabbah. As to the propositions, approximately 42 percent of the sequences are joined within a logic that is substantive: thematic, propositional, or teleological, and 58 percent are joined within a logic that is in no way substantive but narrowly formal: fixed associative. Long stretches of materials join together only because they refer to sequential clauses of verses or sequences of verses, some of them drawn from other books of the Hebrew Scriptures, many of them, of course, drawn from the book of Ruth. This is not a "commentary" to the book of Ruth, but the document is laid out so that it appears to be just that. For Ruth Rabbah, with 60 percent of its composites appealing to the logic of fixed association and 40 percent to propositional logic of one or the other type, we may say that the document appeals to two logics for joining compositions into composites.

So two principles of logical discourse are at play in drawing together the materials our compilers have selected or made up. For the statement of propositions, sizable arguments and proofs, the usual philosophical logic dictates the joining of sentence to sentences and the composition of paragraphs, that is, completed thoughts. For the presentation of the whole, the other logic, the one deriving from imputed, fixed associations, external to the propositions at hand, predominates, though not decisively. The framers of Ruth Rabbah drew together the results of work which people prior to their own labors already had completed, and some of these results they formed into larger compositions – that is, propositional statements – and some into (mere) composites.

Topical Program

Three categories contain the topical and propositional messages of the document, as follows:

ISRAEL AND GOD: Israel's relationship with God encompasses the matter of the covenant, the Torah, and the Land of Israel, all of which bring to concrete and material expression the nature and standing of that relationship. This is a topic treated only casually by our compilers. They make a perfectly standard point. It is that Israel suffers because of sin (I:i). The famine in the time of the judges was because of Israel's rebellion: "My children are rebellious. But as to exterminating them, that is not possible, and to bring them back to Egypt is not possible, and to trade them for some other nation is something I cannot do. But this shall I do for them: lo, I shall torment them with suffering and afflict them with famine in the days when the judges judge" (III:i). This was because they got overconfident (III:ii).

Sometimes God saves Israel on account of its merit, sometimes for his own name's sake (X:i). God's punishment of Israel is always proportionate and appropriate, so LXXIV:i: "Just as in the beginning, Israel gave praise for the redemption: 'This is my God and I will glorify him' (Ex. 15:2), now it is for the substitution [of false gods for God]: 'Thus they exchanged their glory for the likeness of an ox that eats grass' (Ps. 106:20). You have nothing so repulsive and disgusting and strange as an ox when it is eating grass. In the beginning they would effect acquisition through the removal of the sandal, as it is said, 'Now this was the custom in former times in Israel concerning redeeming and exchanging: to confirm a transaction, the one drew off his sandal and gave it to the other, and this was the manner of attesting in Israel.' But now it is by means of the rite of cutting off." None of this forms a centerpiece of interest, and all of it complements the principal points of the writing.

ISRAEL AND THE NATIONS: Israel's relationship with the nations is treated with interest in Israel's history, past, present, and future, and how that cyclical pattern is to be known. This topic is not addressed at all. Only one nation figures in a consequential way, and that is Moab. Under these circumstances we can hardly generalize and say that Moab stands for everybody outside of Israel. That is precisely the opposite of the fact. Moab stands for a problem within Israel, the Messiah from the periphery; and the solution to the problem lies within Israel and not in its relationships to the other, the nations.

ISRAEL ON ITS OWN: Israel on its own concerns the holy nation's understanding of itself: who is Israel, who is not? Within the same rubric we find consideration of Israel's capacity to naturalize the outsider, so to define itself as to extend its own limits, and other questions of self-definition. And, finally, when Israel considers itself, a principal concern is the nature of leadership, for the leader stands for and embodies the people. Therein lies the paradox of the base document and the Midrash compilation alike: How can the leader most wanted, the Messiah, come, as a matter of fact, from the excluded people and not from the holy people?

And, more to the point (for ours is not an accusatory document), how is the excluded included? And in what way do peripheral figures find their way to the center? Phrased in this way, the question yields the obvious answer: through the Torah as embodied by the sage, anybody can become Israel, and any Israelite can find his way to the center. Even more – since it is through Ruth that the Moabite becomes the Israelite, and since (for sages) the mother's status dictates the child's, we may go so far as to say that it is through the Torah that the woman may become a man (at least, in theory). But in stating matters in this way, I have gone beyond my representation of the topical and propositional program. Let us review it from the beginning to the end.

The sin of Israel, which caused the famine, was that it was judging its own judges. "He further said to the Israelites, 'So God says to Israel, "I have given a share of glory to the judges and I have called them gods, and they humiliate them. Woe to a generation that judges its judges"'" (I:i). The Israelites were slothful in burying Joshua, and that showed disrespect to their leader (II:i). They were slothful about repentance in the time of the judges, and that is what caused the famine; excess of commitment to one's own affairs leads to sin. The Israelites did not honor the prophets (III:iii). The old have to bear with the young, and the young with the old, or Israel will go into exile (IV:i). The generation that judges its leadership ("judges") will be penalized (V:i). Arrogance to the authority of the Torah is penalized (V:i). Elimelech was punished because he broke the penalized heart; everyone depended upon him, and he proved undependable (V:iii); so bad leadership will destroy Israel. Why was Elimelech punished? It is because he broke the Israelites' heart. When the years of drought came, his maid went out into the marketplace, with her basket in her hand. So the people of the town said, "Is this the one on whom we depended, that he can provide for the whole town with ten years of food? Lo, his maid is standing in the marketplace with her basket in her hand!" So Elimelech was one of the great men of the town and one of those who sustained the generation. But when the years of famine came, he said, "Now all the Israelites are going to come knocking on my door, each with his basket." The leadership of a community is its glory: "The great man of a town – he is its splendor, he is its glory, he is its praise. When he has turned from there, so, too, have turned its splendor, glory, and praise" (XI:i.1C).

A distinct but fundamental component of the theory of Israel concerns who is Israel and how one becomes a part of Israel. That theme, of course, proves fundamental to our document, so much of which is preoccupied with how Ruth can be the progenitor of the Messiah, deriving as she does not only from gentile but from Moabite stock. Israel's history follows rules that are to be learned in Scripture; nothing is random and all things are connected (IV:ii). The fact that the king of Moab honored God explains why God raised up from Moab "a son who will sit on the throne of the Lord" (VIII:i.3). The proselyte is discouraged but then accepted. Thus XVI:i.2B: "People are to turn a proselyte away. But if he is insistent beyond that point, he is accepted. A person should always push away with the left hand while offering encouragement with the right." Orpah, who left Naomi, was rewarded for the little that she did for her, but she was raped when she left her (XVIII:i.1-3). When Orpah went back to her people, she went back to her gods (XIX:i).

Ruth's intention to convert was absolutely firm, and Naomi laid out all the problems for her, but she acceded to every condition (XX:i). Thus she said, "Under all circumstances I intend to convert, but it is better that it be through your action and not through that of another." When Naomi heard her say this, she began laying out for her the laws that govern proselytes. She said to her, "My daughter, it is not the way of Israelite women to go to theaters and circuses put on by idolators." She said to her, "Where you go I will go." She said to her, "My daughter, it is not the way of Israelite women to live in a house that lacks a mezuzah." She said to her, "Where you lodge I will lodge." "Your people shall be my people": This refers to the penalties and admonitions against sinning. "And your God my God": This refers to the other religious duties. And so onward: "for where you go I will go": to the tent of meeting, Gilgal, Shiloh, Nob, Gibeon, and the eternal house. "And where you lodge I will lodge": "I shall spend the night concerned about the offerings." "Your people shall be my people": "so nullifying my idol." "And your God my God": "to pay a full recompense for my action." I find here the centerpiece of the compilation and its principal purpose. The same message is at XXI:i.1-3.

Proselytes are respected by God, so XXII:i: "And when Naomi saw that she was determined to go with her, [she said no more]": Said R. Judah b. R. Simon, "Notice how precious are proselytes before the Omnipresent. Once she had decided to convert, the Scripture treats her as equivalent to Naomi." Boaz, for his part, was equally virtuous and free of sins (XXVI:i). The law provided for the conversion of Ammonite and Moabite women, but not Ammonite and Moabite men, so the acceptance of Ruth the Moabite was fully in accord with the law, and anyone who did not know that fact was an ignoramus (XXVI:i.4, among many passages). An Israelite hero who came from Ruth and Boaz was David, who was a great master of the Torah, thus: "he was 'skillful in playing, and a mighty man of war, prudent in affairs, good-looking, and the Lord is with him' (1 Sam. 16:18)": "Skillful in playing": in Scripture. "and a mighty man of valor": in Mishnah. "A man of war": who knows the give and take of the war of the Torah. "Prudent in affairs": in good deeds. "Good-looking": in Talmud. "Prudent in affairs": able to reason deductively. "Good-looking": enlightened in law. "And the Lord is with him": the law accords with his opinions.

Ruth truly accepted Judaism upon the instruction, also, of Boaz (XXXIV:i), thus: "Then Boaz said to Ruth, 'Now listen, my daughter, do not go to glean in another field'": This is on the strength of the verse, "You shall have no other gods before me" (Ex. 20:3). "'Or leave this one':" This is on the strength of the verse, "This is my God and I will glorify him" (Ex. 15:2). "But keep close to my maidens": This speaks of the righteous, who are called maidens: "Will you play with him as with a bird, or will you bind him for your maidens" (Job 40:29). The glosses invest the statement with a vast tapestry of meaning. Boaz speaks to Ruth as a Jew by choice, and the entire exchange is now typological. Note also the typological meanings imputed at XXXV:i.1-5. Ruth had prophetic power (XXXVI:ii). Ruth was rewarded for her sincere conversion by Solomon (XXXVIII:i.1).

Taking shelter under the wings of the Presence of God, which is what the convert does, is the greatest merit accorded to all who do deeds of grace, thus: So notice the power of the righteous and the power of righteousness, the power of those who do deeds of grace. For they take shelter not in the shadow of the dawn, nor in the shadow of the wings of the earth, nor in the shadow of the wings of the sun, nor in the shadow of the wings of the hayyot, nor in the shadow of the wings of the cherubim or the seraphim. But under whose wings do they take shelter? "They take shelter under the shadow of the One at whose word the world was created: 'How precious is your loving kindness O God, and the children of men take refuge in the shadow of your wings' (Ps. 36:8)."

The language that Boaz used to Ruth, "Come here," bore with it deeper reference to six: David, Solomon, the throne as held by the Davidic monarchy, and ultimately, the Messiah, for example, in the following instance: "The fifth interpretation refers to the Messiah: 'Come here': means, to the throne. "'And eat some bread': this is the bread of the throne. "'And dip your morsel in vinegar': this refers to suffering: 'But he was wounded because of our transgressions' (Isa. 53:5). "'So she sat beside the reapers': for the throne is destined to be taken from him for a time: 'For I will gather all nations against Jerusalem to battle and the city shall be taken' (Zech. 14:2). "'And he passed to her parched grain': for he will be restored to the throne: 'And he shall smite the land with the rod of his mouth' (Isa. 11:4)." R. Berekhiah in the name of R. Levi: "As was the first redeemer, so is the last redeemer: 'Just as the first redeemer was revealed and then hidden from them, so the last redeemer will be revealed to them and then hidden from them.'" (XL:i.1ff.).

Boaz instructed Ruth on how to be a proper Israelite woman, so LIII:i: "Wash yourself": from the filth of idolatry that is yours. "And anoint yourself": this refers to the religious deeds and acts of righteousness [that are required of an Israelite]. "And put on your best clothes": this refers to her Sabbath clothing. So did Naomi encompass Ruth within Israel: "and go down to the threshing floor": She said to her, "My merit will go down there with you." Moab, whence Ruth came, was conceived not for the sake of fornication but for the sake of Heaven (LV:i.1B). Boaz, for his part, was a master of the Torah and when he ate and drank, that formed a typology for his study of the Torah (LVI:i). His was a life of grace, Torah study, and marriage for holy purposes. Whoever trusts in God is exalted, and that refers to Ruth and Boaz; God put it in his heart to bless her (LVII:i). David sang Psalms to thank God for his grandmother, Ruth, so LIX:i.5, "[At midnight I will rise to give thanks to you] because of your righteous judgments" (Ps. 119:62): [David speaks,] "The acts of judgment that you brought upon the Ammonites and Moabites." "And the righteous deeds that you carried out for my grandfather and my grandmother [Boaz, Ruth, of whom David speaks here]." "For had he hastily cursed her but once, where should I have come from? But you put in his heart the will to bless her: 'And he said, "May you be blessed by the Lord."'" Because of the merit of the six measures that Boaz gave Ruth, six righteous persons came forth from him, each with six virtues: David, Hezekiah, Josiah, Hananiah, Mishael, Azariah [counted as one], Daniel and the royal Messiah.

God facilitated the union of Ruth and Boaz (LXVIII:i). Boaz's relative was ignorant for not knowing that while a male Moabite was excluded, a female one was acceptable for marriage. The blessing of Boaz was, "May all the children you have come from this righteous woman" (LXXIX:i), and that is precisely the blessing accorded to Isaac and to Elkanah. God made Ruth an ovary, which she had lacked (LXXX:i). Naomi was blessed with Messianic blessings (LXXXI:i), thus: "Then the women said to Naomi, 'Blessed be the Lord, who has not left you this day without next of kin; and may his name be renowned in Israel':" Just as "this day" rules dominion in the firmament, so will your descendants rule and govern Israel forever. On account of the blessings of the women, the line of David was not wholly exterminated in the time of Athaliah.

David was ridiculed because he was descended from Ruth, the Moabitess, so LXXXV:i. But many other distinguished families derived from humble origins, so David said, "Said David before the Holy One, blessed be He, 'How long will they rage against me and say, "Is his family not invalid [for marriage into Israel]? Is he not descended from Ruth the Moabitess?"'" "'Commune with your own heart upon your bed': [David continues,] 'You, too, have you not descended from two sisters? You look at your own origins "and shut up."'" "'So Tamar who married your ancestor Judah – is she not of an invalid family? But she was only a descendant of Shem, son of Noah. So do you come from such impressive genealogy?'" David referred to and defended his Moabite origins, so LXXXIX:i: "Then I said, 'Lo, I have come [in the roll of the book it is written of me]' (Ps. 40:8). [David says,] 'Then I had to recite a song when I came, for the word "then" refers only to a song, as it is said, "Then sang Moses" (Ex. 15:1).'" "'I was covered by the verse, "An Ammonite and a Moabite shall not come into the assembly of the Lord" (Deut. 23:4), but I have come "In the roll of the book it is written of me" (Ps. 40:8).'" "in the roll": this refers to the verse, [David continues], "concerning whom you commanded that they should not enter into your congregation" (Lam. 1:10). "Of the book it is written of me": "An Ammonite and a Moabite shall not enter into the assembly of the Lord" (Deut. 23:4). "It is not enough that I have come, but in the roll and the book it is written concerning me": "In the roll": Perez, Hezron, Ram, Amminadab, Nahshon, Salmon, Boaz, Obed, Jesse, David. "In the book": "And the Lord said, Arise, anoint him, for this is he" (1 Sam. 16:12).

II. Unarticulated Premises: The Givens of Religious Conduct

Nothing qualifies here.

III. Unarticulated Premises: The Givens of Religious Conviction

1.   Famine comes about because of failure to do God's work, sloth in the time of Joshua, excess commitment to one's own affairs, sloth in the time of Elijah in repenting, and the same in the time of the Judges:

II

I.1   A.   "And it came to pass in the days when the judges ruled":

       B.   "Slothfulness casts into a deep sleep, and an idle person will suffer hunger. [He who keeps the commandment keeps his life; he who despises the word will die]" (Prov. 19:15-16):

       C.   ["Slothfulness casts into a deep sleep"] because the Israelites were slothful about burying Joshua:

       D.   "And they buried him in the border of his inheritance...on the north of the mountain of Gaash" (Josh. 24:30).

       E.   Said R. Berekhiah, "We have reviewed the entire Scripture and have found no place called Gaash.

       F.   "What is the meaning of 'the mountain of Gaash'?

       G.   "It is that the Israelites were preoccupied [a word that uses the same consonants as the word Gaash] so that they were slothful about burying Joshua.

H.   "[Why was that the case? Because] at that time the land of Israel was being divided up, and the parceling out was too important to them.

I.   "The Israelites were occupied with their own work. This one was occupied with his field, and that one was occupied with his vineyard, and the other with his olives, and the other with his stone quarry. Thus: 'and an idle person will suffer hunger.'

J.   "So the Israelites were slothful about burying Joshua.

K.   "The Holy One, blessed be He, wanted to cause an earthquake to come upon the inhabitants of the world: 'Then the earth did shake [a word that uses the same consonants as the word for mount Gaash] and quake' (Ps. 18:8).

I.2   A.   "...and an idle person will suffer hunger":

B.   It is because they were deceiving the Holy One, blessed be He.

C.   Some of them were worshiping idols.

D.   Therefore he starved them of the Holy Spirit [as in the continuation of the intersecting verse, "He who keeps the commandment keeps his life; he who despises the word will die"]:

E.   "And the word of the Lord was precious in those days."

I.3   A.   Another interpretation of the verse, "Slothfulness casts into a deep sleep, and an idle person will suffer hunger. [He who keeps the commandment keeps his life; he who despises the word will die]" (Prov. 19:15-16):

B.   ["Slothfulness casts into a deep sleep"] because the Israelites were slothful about repenting in the time of Elijah.

C.   "...casts into a deep sleep": prophecy increased.

D.   But the verse says, "causes to fall," [meaning, prophecy decreased] and you say that it increased?

E.   It is in line with the saying, "the market for fruit has fallen" [because a lot of fruit has come to the market for sale, the price of fruit has gone down].

F.   Said R. Simon, "It is like someone who says to his fellow, 'Here is the bag, the money, the measure; go eat.'"

I.6   A.   "...and an idle person will suffer hunger":

B.   It is because they were deceiving the Holy One, blessed be He.

C.   Some of them were worshiping idols, and some of them were worshiping the Holy One, blessed be He.

D.   That is in line with what Elijah said to them, "How long will you halt between two opinions" (1 Kgs. 18:21).

I.7   A.   "...will suffer hunger":

B.   a famine in the days of Elijah: "As the Lord of hosts lives, before whom I stand" (1 Kgs. 18:15).

I.8   A.   Another interpretation of the verse, "Slothfulness casts into a deep sleep, [and an idle person will suffer hunger]":

B.   ["Slothfulness casts into a deep sleep"] because the Israelites were slothful about repentance in the time of the Judges,

C.   they were "cast into a deep sleep."

I.9   A.   "...and an idle person will suffer hunger":

B.   Because they were deceiving the Holy One, blessed be He: some of them were worshiping idols, and some of them were worshiping the Holy One, blessed be He,

C.   the Holy One, blessed be He, brought a famine in the days of their judges:

D.   [Supply: "And it came to pass in the days when the judges ruled, there was a famine in the land."]

IV. Matters of Philosophy, Natural Science and Metaphysics

I find nothing remotely pertinent.

10

Ruth Rabbah Parashah One

The parashah yields nothing both fresh and important.

11

Ruth Rabbah Parashah Two

I. Unarticulated Premises: The Givens of Religious Conduct

Some halakhic rules occur, but none is analyzed as to its premises.

II. Unarticulated Premises: The Givens of Religious Conviction

1. Heaven values matters differently from the way men do, and who is low here is valued on high:

XXI

I.5   A.   R. Miaha son of the son of R. Joshua fell unconscious from illness for three days, and then three days later he regained consciousness.

B.   His father said to him, "What did you see?"

C.   He said to him, "In a world that was mixed up I found myself."

D.   He said to him, "And what did you see there?"

E.   He said to him, "Many people I saw who here are held in honor and there in contempt."

F.   When R. Yohanan and R. Simeon b. Laqish heard, they came in to visit him. The father said to them, "Did you hear what this boy said?"

G.   They said to him, "What?"

H.   He told them the incident.

I.   R. Simeon b. Laqish said, "And is this not an explicit verse of Scripture? 'Thus says the Lord God, the mitre shall be removed, and the crown taken off; this shall be no more the same; that which is low shall be exalted, and that which is high abased' (Ezek. 21:31)."

J.   Said R. Yohanan, "Had I come here only to hear this matter, it would have sufficed."

III. Matters of Philosophy, Natural Science and Metaphysics

Nothing belongs here.

12

Ruth Rabbah Parashah Three

The parashah contains nothing relevant to our study.

13

Ruth Rabbah Parashah Four

I find nothing relevant to our study.

14

Ruth Rabbah Parashah Five

This parashah contributes nothing to our inquiry.

15

Ruth Rabbah Parashah Six

I discern here no contributions to our study.

16

Ruth Rabbah Parashah Seven

I. Unarticulated Premises: The Givens of Religious Conduct

While at LXXIV:i there is extensive discussion of the rites of removing the shoe and levirate marriage, I see no discussion of the matter that appeals to a prior premise or presupposition of note.

II. Unarticulated Premises: The Givens of Religious Conviction

There is nothing that requires our attention.

III. Matters of Philosophy, Natural Science and Metaphysics

This category of course is hopeless here.

17

Ruth Rabbah Parashah Eight

The parashah contributes nothing of interest.

Part Three

ESTHER RABBAH I

18

Esther Rabbah I Petihtaot

I. The Character of Esther Rabbah I

In Esther Rabbah Part One (that is, covering the book of Esther's first two chapters), we find only one message, and it is reworked in only a few ways. It is that the nations are swine, their rulers fools, and Israel is subjugated to them, though it should not be, because of its own sins. But just as God saved Israel in the past, so the salvation that Israel can attain will recapitulate the former ones. On the stated theme, Israel among the nations, sages propose a proposition entirely familiar from the books of Deuteronomy through Kings, on the one side, and much of prophetic literature, on the other.

The proposition is familiar, and so is the theme; but since the book of Esther can hardly be characterized as "Deuteronomic," lacking all interest in the covenant, the land, and issues of atonement (beyond the conventional sackcloth, ashes, and fasting, hardly the fodder for prophetic regeneration and renewal!), the sages' distinctive viewpoint in the document must be deemed an original and interesting contribution of their own. But the message is somewhat more complicated than merely a negative judgment against the nations. If I have to identify one recurrent motif that captures that theology, it is the critical role of Esther and Mordecai, particularly Mordecai, who, as sage, emerges in the position of messiah. And that is a message that is particular to the exposition of the book of Esther's opening chapters.

Gender defines the focus for both documents, yielding the opposite of what is anticipated. Ruth Rabbah has the Messiah born of an outsider, Esther Rabbah has salvation come of a woman. For Esther and Mordecai, woman and the sage Messiah, function in this document in much the same way that Ruth and David, woman and sage Messiah, work in Ruth Rabbah. While the sages of Ruth Rabbah face their own, distinctive problem, the way the outsider becomes the insider, the Moabite Messiah, yet, Ruth Rabbah and Esther Rabbah Part One deal with the same fundamental fact: the Messiah sage dictates the future of Israel, because he (never she) realizes the rule of the Torah. In Esther Rabbah Part One many things say one thing: the Torah dictates Israel's fate, if you want to know what that fate will be, study the Torah, and if you want to control that fate, follow the model of the sage Messiah.

Logic of Coherent Discourse

The entire document is made up of free-standing compositions, made cogent within themselves mainly by propositions but sometimes by teleological logic, and made coherent beginning to end principally by reference to the same shared and fixed association with a common document.

	Number	Percent of the Whole
Propositional and Philosophical Discourse	12	26%
Themes Worked out by Teleology Expressed in Narrative	3	12%
The Logic of Fixed Association	23	50%
The Cogency of a Fixed Analytical Method	0	0%
No Clear Coherence between or among Successive Units of Completed Discourse	7	15%
Not Relevant to the Issue	1	—

If we now ask about the operative logics, that is, the first three entries, the result is as follows:

	Number	Percent
Propositional and Philosophical Discourse and Themes Worked out by Teleology Expressed in Narrative	15	39%
The Logic of Fixed Association	23	61%

These results are familiar. For the statement of propositions, sizable arguments and proofs, the usual philosophical logic dictates the joining of sentence to sentences and the composition of paragraphs, that is, completed thoughts. For the presentation of the whole, the other logic, the one deriving from imputed, fixed associations, external to the propositions at hand, predominates, though not decisively.

Topical Program

These episodic propositions comprise the document's single message. Bad government comes about because of the sins of the people (VII:i). But that proposition is realized in discourse mainly about bad government by the nations, and, given the base document, that is hardly surprising. God was neglected by the people, so he is left solitary through his own actions, which responded to the people's actions (XVIII:iii). This serves Lamentations Rabbah as its Petihta 10; but the proposition surely is not alien to our base document. The contrast between the relative neglect of this inviting topic and the intense interest in another, the one that follows, which characterize Esther Rabbah Part One, and the opposite emphases and interests revealed in Lamentations Rabbah, is readily discerned.

Our compilation concentrates upon this one subject, and all of its important messages present the same proposition, in several parts. Israel's life among the nations is a sequence of sorrows, each worse than the former: "In the morning, you shall say, 'Would it were evening!' and at evening you shall say, 'Would it were morning!' 'In the morning,' of Babylonia, you shall say, 'Would it were evening!'" But through Torah, Israel can break the cycle: Said R. Simeon b. Yohai, "You can acquire rights of ownership to members of the nations of the world, as it says, 'Moreover of the children of the strangers that sojourn among you, of them may you buy' (Lev. 25:45), but they cannot acquire rights of ownership to you. Why not? Because you acquired 'these the words of the covenant.' And the nations? They did not acquire 'these the words of the covenant' ['These are the words of the covenant']" (I:i.4-11). When Israel is subjugated by the nations, God will not spurn, abhor, destroy them or break his covenant with them – in the age of Babylonia, Media, the Greeks, and the wicked kingdom; of Vespasian, Trajan, Haman, the Romans (II:i.1). The same is repeated at III:i.1-5.

In comparing the ages through which the Jews had lived, Babylonian, Median, Greek, Roman, the same position recurs. When the righteous achieve great power, there is joy in the world, and when the wicked achieve great power, there is groaning in the world; this is so of Israelite and gentile kings (IV:i). Gentile kings may do good things or bad things (VI:i). But even the good kings are not without flaws. When a bad king rules, it is because of the sins of the people, those who will not do the will of the creator (VII:i). God worked through whomever he chose. From the beginning of the creation of the world, the Holy One, blessed be He, designated for every one what was suitable. Ahasuerus the first of those who sell [people at a price], Haman the first of those who buy [people at a price] (VIII:i). There are decisions made by God that determine the life of nations and individuals; Israel's history follows rules that can be learned in Scripture; nothing is random, all things are connected, and fundamental laws of history dictate the meaning of what happens among the nations (VIII:ii).

Ultimately, God will destroy Israel's enemies (IX:i). God will save Israel when not a shred of merit will be found among the nations of the world (X:i.15). The prosperity of the nations is only for a time; then the nations will be punished and Israel redeemed (XI:i). There will be full recompense, and the contrast between Israel's subjugation and the nations' prosperity will be resolved. The principle of measure for measure governs. Pagan kings propose to do what God himself does not claim to be able to do. But in the age to come, God will accomplish the union of opposites, which in this time pagan kings claim to be able to do but cannot accomplish (XVII:i). Pagan kings rebel against not only God but also their own gods (XVIII:i). But for the slightest gesture of respect for God they are rewarded (XVIII:i).

God is in full control of everyone at all times. The salvation in the time of Ahasuerus was directly linked, detail by detail, to the punishment in the time of Nebuchadnezzar (XVIII:ii). Israel's relationship with one empire is no different from its relationship to the other. The same base verse, Ps. 10:14, accounts for both Rome and Iran. The relationship of each to Israel is the same. Both of them call into question Israel's faith in the power of God by showing off their own power. Esau/Romulus and Remus pay back God's blessing by building temples of idolatry in Rome. Belshazzar/Vashti/Iran do the same by oppressing Israel. Both intend by their power to prove that they are stronger than God. But, the premise of course maintains, God will show in the end who is the stronger. The upshot is to underline the irony that derives from the contrast between the empires' power and God's coming display of his power; that and one other thing: the challenge facing God in showing his power over theirs (XVIII:iv).

Israel possesses wise men, the nations' sages are fools thus: "'The impious man destroys his neighbor through speech': this refers to the seven princes of Persia and Media. 'But through their knowledge the righteous are rescued': this refers to the portion of Issachar." (XXIII:i). We have at XXIII:II three sets of explanations for the seven names, all of them working with the letters of the respective names and imputing to them other meanings sustained by the same consonants. The first set of explanations deals with the tasks each of the princes carried out in the palace, feeding the king. The next deals with the rites of the Temple that each name stands for; here the princes are given a good task, which is to thwart the advice of Haman. But the upshot is to match feeding the wicked (or stupid) king, Ahasuerus, as against tending the King of kings of kings, God. And the third set of explanations then assigns to the seven the punishment that is owing to the wicked government that has endangered the lives of the Jews. So three distinct, and yet complementary, hermeneutical interests coincide: pagan government and the feeding of pagan kings, divine government and the counterpart, which is the Temple cult, and, finally, God's punishment for the pagan government. While, it goes without saying, each set of seven names can stand on its own, it seems to me clear that the compositor has appealed to a single cogent program in order to accomplish what I see as a beautiful piece of sustained and coherent exposition, one that makes a variety of distinct components of a single important proposition. I cannot imagine a finer execution of the exposition of details aimed at registering a major conception.

There is a correspondence between how Israel suffers and how the nations prosper, so XXVIII:i: "With the language with which the throne was taken away from her [Esther's] ancestor, when Samuel said to him, 'And he has given it to a neighbor of yours, who is better than you' (1 Sam. 15:28), with that same language, the throne was given back to him: 'let the king give her royal position to another who is better than she.'" Saul lost the throne because he did not destroy Amalek, Esther got it back because she did. Obedience to divine instructions made the difference. Persian women suffered and were humiliated because they had ridiculed Israelite women (XXXIV:i).

Those who do righteousness at all times are going to be the ones who will carry out God's salvation, thus: "When Haman wanted to exterminate Israel and weighed out ten thousand pieces of silver to those who were to do the work for Ahasuerus, it is written, 'And I will pay ten thousand talents of silver into the hands...'"(Est. 3:9), what is then written? "Now there was a Jew in Susa the capital whose name was Mordecai, son of Jair, son of Shimei, son of Kish, a Benjaminite." Simon, p. 72, n. 7: Mordecai is connected with David by being ascribed to the tribe of Judah. The point is that they that do righteousness at all times, that is, Mordecai, are to be remembered when God's salvation is required and it is performed through them. Accordingly, Mordecai in his generation was equivalent to Moses in his generation: "Now the man Moses was very meek" (Num. 12:3). Just as Moses stood in the breach, "Therefore he said that he would destroy them, had not Moses, his chosen one, stood before him in the breach" (Ps. 106:23), so did Mordecai: "Seeking the good of his people and speaking peace to all his seed" (Est. 10:3). Just as Moses taught Torah to Israel, "Behold, I have taught you statutes and ordinances" (Deut. 4:5), so Mordecai did: "And he sent letters...with words of peace and truth" (Est. 9:30), [and truth refers to Torah:] "Buy the truth and do not sell it" (Prov. 23:23).

God always responds to Israel's need. The reason this point is pertinent here is the repeated contrast, also, of Mordecai and Haman; the upshot is that ultimately Israel gets what it has coming just as do the nations; and when Israel gets its redemption, it is through people of a single sort, Moses, Abraham, Mordecai. The redemptions of Israel in times past then provide the model and paradigm for what is going to happen in the future. None of this has any bearing on the land and nothing invokes the covenant, which is why I see the entire matter in the present context. When God saves Israel, it is always in response to how they have been punished, thus at XXXVIII:i.9: R. Berekiah in the name of R. Levi said, "Said the Holy One, blessed be He, to the Israelites, 'You have wept, saying, "We have become orphans and fatherless" (Lam. 5:3). By your lives, I shall raise up for you in Media a savior whom will have no father and no mother.' Thus: 'for she had neither father nor mother.'" If the mortal king remembers and pays back, how much the more so will God (LIV:i).

As to Israel's distinctive leadership and its life within its own boundaries, the nature of our base document, with its concern for its heroes, Mordecai and Esther, secures for this subject a more than negligible place in the propositional program of our compilation. Israel's leadership consistently follows the same norms, and what the ancestors taught, the descendants learn. Thus Esther behaved as had Rachel (LI:i), so: "Now Esther had not made known her kindred or her people, as Mordecai had charged her; [for Esther obeyed Mordecai just as when she was brought up by him]": This teaches that she kept silent like Rachel, her ancestor, who kept silent. All of her great ancestors had kept silent. Rachel kept silent when she saw her wedding band on the hand of her sister but shut up about it. Benjamin, her son, kept silent. You may know that that is so, for the stone that stood for him on the high priest's breastplate was a jasper, indicating that he knew of the sale of Joseph, but he kept silent. [The word for jasper contains letters that stand for] "there is a mouth," [meaning, he could have told], but he kept silent. Saul, from whom she descended: "Concerning the matter of the kingdom he did not tell him" (1 Sam. 10:16). Esther: "Now Esther had not made known her kindred or her people, as Mordecai had charged her." What happens now therefore has already happened, and we know how to respond and what will come in consequence of our deeds.

II. Unarticulated Premises: The Givens of Religious Conduct

There are no halakhic materials that pertain.

III. Unarticulated Premises: The Givens of Religious Conviction

1. Though Israel's history is marked by four successive gentile rulers, the fifth and final monarchy over Israel will be that of the Messiah:

I

I.3 A. [Another interpretation of the verse, "And your life shall hang in doubt before you; night and day you shall be in dread, and have no assurance of your life":]

B. Rab interpreted the verse to speak of the time of Haman.

C. "'And your life shall hang in doubt before you': this speaks of the twenty-four hours from the removal of the ring.

D. "'night and day you shall be in dread': this speaks of the time that the letters were sent forth.

E. "'and have no assurance of your life': this was when the enemies of the Jews were told to be 'ready against that day' (Est. 3:14)."

I.4 A. "In the morning, you shall say, 'Would it were evening!' and at evening you shall say, 'Would it were morning!'":

B. "In the morning," of Babylonia, "you shall say, 'Would it were evening!'"

C. "In the morning," of Media, "you shall say, 'Would it were evening!'"

D. "In the morning," of Greece, "you shall say, 'Would it were evening!'"

E. "In the morning," of Edom, "you shall say, 'Would it were evening!'"

I.5 A. Another interpretation of the verse: "In the morning, you shall say, 'Would it were evening!' and at evening you shall say, 'Would it were morning!'":

B. "In the morning" of Babylonia, "you shall say, 'Would it were the evening of Media!'"

C. "In the morning," of Media, "you shall say, 'Would it were evening of Greece!'"

D. "In the morning," of Greece, "you shall say, 'Would it were evening of Edom!'"

E. Why so? "because of the dread which your heart shall fear and the sights which your eyes shall see."

Nonetheless, God remains with Israel and will ultimately stand by them and redeem them from their enemies:

II

I.1 A. Samuel commenced by citing the following verse of Scripture: "Yet for all that, when they are in the land of their enemies, I will not spurn them, neither will I abhor them so as to destroy them utterly and break my covenant with them, for I am the Lord their God; but I will for their sake remember the covenant with their forefathers, whom I brought forth out of the land of Egypt in the sight of the nations, that I might be their God: I am the Lord" (Lev. 26:44-45):

B. "'I will not spurn them': in Babylonia.

C.   "'neither will I abhor them': in Media.
D.   "'so as to destroy them utterly': under Greek rule.
E.   "'and break my covenant with them': under the wicked kingdom.
F.   "'for I am the Lord their God': in the age to come."
G.   Taught R. Hiyya, "'I will not spurn them': in the time of Vespasian.
H.   "'neither will I abhor them': in the time of Trajan.
I.   "'so as to destroy them utterly': in the time of Haman.
J.   "'and break my covenant with them': in the time of the Romans.
K.   "'for I am the Lord their God': in the time of Gog and Magog."

IV. Matters of Philosophy, Natural Science and Metaphysics

Nothing in the *petihtaot* belongs here.

19

Esther Rabbah I Parashah One

I. Unarticulated Premises: The Givens of Religious Conduct

No halakhic matters arise.

II. Unarticulated Premises: The Givens of Religious Conviction

1. God and the angels decide what will happen on earth and determine the course of events:

XI

I.1   A.   "In those days when King Ahasuerus sat on his royal throne in Susa the capital":

       B.   This is one of the occasions on which the ministering angels wrote out complaints before the Holy One, blessed be He.

       C.   For they were saying before him, "Lord of the world, the house of the sanctuary is destroyed, and this wicked man is sitting and making a party!"

       D.   Said he to them, "Days will match days [and there will be recompense in full measure]."

       E.   That is in line with the following verse of Scripture: "In those days I saw in Judah some treading wine presses on the Sabbath" (Neh. 13:15). [Simon, p. 25, n. 5: And this was in the days of Artaxerxes/ Ahasuerus....The troubles which came upon the Jews, of which the king's banquet was the starting point, were a punishment for the desecration of the Sabbath.]

II.1   A.   Said R. Aibu, "It is written, 'For the kingdom is the Lord's and he is the ruler over the nations' (Ps. 22:29).

       B.   "And yet you say here, 'when King Ahasuerus sat on his royal throne'?

       C.   "In the past dominion reigned in Israel, but when they sinned, its dominion was taken away from them and given to the nations of the world.

       D.   "That is in line with the following verse of Scripture: 'I will give the land over into the hand of evil men' (Ezek. 30:12)."

E.   R. Isaac explained this verse, "Into the hand of evil stewards."

F.   [Continuing D:] "In the future, when the Israelites repent, the Holy One, blessed be He, will take dominion from the nations of the world and restore it to Israel.

G.   "When will this come about? 'When saviors will come up on Mount Zion' (Obad. 1:21)."

III. Matters of Philosophy, Natural Science and Metaphysics

Nothing comes under consideration here.

20

Esther Rabbah I Parashah Two

I. Unarticulated Premises: The Givens of Religious Conduct

Nothing pertains.

II. Unarticulated Premises: The Givens of Religious Conviction

The only source of honor is study of the Torah; money is a poor second:

XI

I.14   A.   R. Simeon b. Yohai had a friend who lived nearby in Tyre.

        B.   One day he came to him. He heard his servant saying to him, "What are we going to eat today, thin lentil soup or thick lentil soup?"

        C.   He said to him, "Thin."

        D.   He began talking with him, and the friend noticed [and realized he had overheard the conversation. Therefore] he sent word to his household: "Get out for him all those silver dishes."

        E.   He said to him, "Will my Lord pay me the honor of drinking with me today?"

        F.   He said to him, "Yes."

        G.   When he went into his house, he saw all the silver dishes and was surprised. He said to him, "Would someone who has all this money eat thin lentil soup?"

        H.   He said to him, "Indeed so, my lord. As for you, your Torah learning wins you honor, but as for us, the only honor we have is money. Without it no one honors us."

III. Matters of Philosophy, Natural Science and Metaphysics

The category does not apply.

21

Esther Rabbah I Parashah Three

I. Unarticulated Premises: The Givens of Religious Conduct

The category is irrelevant.

II. Unarticulated Premises: The Givens of Religious Conviction

1. God's omnipotence may be called into question by the behavior of the great empires, but that is only just for now. The history of Israel produces matched sets of relationships, with Rome and Iran; each relates to Israel in the same way. They serve to call into question Israel's faith in the power of God, by showing off their own power. Esau/Romulus and Remus pay back God's blessing by building temples to idols. Belshazzar, Vashti, and Iran do the same by oppressing Israel. Both intend to prove they are stronger than God. But God shows in the end who is the stronger. The empires display power, but God will display much greater power in time to come:

XVIII

IV.1   A. It is written, "You have seen, for you behold trouble and vexation, to pay them back with your hand; unto you the helpless commits himself. You have been the helper of the fatherless" (Ps. 10:14).

       B. Said the community of Israel before the Holy One, blessed be He, "Lord of the world, 'you have seen' that the wicked Esau has come and is going to destroy the house of the sanctuary and exile the Israelites from their land and lead them away in iron collars.

       C. "'for you behold trouble and vexation, to pay them back with your hand': You caused your presence to dwell upon Isaac, so that he said to Esau, 'Behold, of the fat places of the earth shall be your dwelling...and by your sword you shall live' (Gen. 27:39).

       D. "'unto you the helpless commits himself': 'Tomorrow he is going to come and take orphans and widows and lock them up in prison and say to them, "Let the one of whom it is written, 'he is the father of the fatherless and judge in behalf of widows' (Ps. 68:6) come and save you from my power.""'"

E. "But truly 'You have been the helper of the fatherless':

F. "There were two who were left as orphans to Esau, Remus and Romulus, and you allowed a she-wolf to give them suck, and in the end they went and built two enormous tents in Rome."

IV.2 A. Another explanation of the verse, "You have seen, for you behold trouble and vexation, to pay them back with your hand; unto you the helpless commits himself. You have been the helper of the fatherless" (Ps. 10:14).

B. Said the community of Israel before the Holy One, blessed be He, "Lord of the world, 'you have seen' that Nebuchadnezzar, that wicked man has come and is going to destroy the house of the sanctuary and exile the Israelites from their land and lead them away in iron collars.

C. "'for you behold trouble and vexation, to pay them back with your hand': You caused your presence to dwell upon Jeremiah, so he said to us, 'And all the nations shall serve him and his son and his son's son' (Jer. 27:7).

D. "'unto you the helpless commits himself': 'Tomorrow he is going to come and take Hananiah, Mishael, and Azariah, and throw them into the hot stove and say to them, "And who is the god who will deliver you out of my power"' (Dan. 3:15).

E. "But truly 'You have been the helper of the fatherless': one orphan was left to him [Vashti is daughter of Belshazzar], and you made her queen over a kingdom that did not even belong to her, and who was it? It was Vashti."

III. Matters of Philosophy, Natural Science and Metaphysics

Nothing of philosophical interest impinges.

22

Esther Rabbah I Parashah Four

The parashah contains nothing of interest.

23

Esther Rabbah I Parashah Five

The parashah contains nothing of interest.

24

Esther Rabbah I Parashah Six

I. Unarticulated Premises: The Givens of Religious Conduct

This category does not serve.

II. Unarticulated Premises: The Givens of Religious Conviction

1. The history of Israel is formed of matching components, for example, not only enemies that correspond to one another, but also leaders and prophets:

XXXVI

II.1   A.   "Now there was a Jewish man in Susa the capital whose name was Mordecai, son of Jair, son of Shimei, son of Kish, a Benjaminite":

      B.   "man":

      C.   This teaches that Mordecai in his generation was equivalent to Moses in his generation: "Now the man Moses was very meek" (Num. 12:3).

      D.   [The comparisons then are as follows:] Just as Moses stood in the breach, "Therefore he said that he would destroy them, had not Moses, his chosen one, stood before him in the breach" (Ps. 106:23), so did Mordecai: "Seeking the good of his people and speaking peace to all his seed" (Est. 10:3).

      E.   Just as Moses taught Torah to Israel, "Behold, I have taught you statutes and ordinances" (Deut. 4:5), so Mordecai did: "And he sent letters...with words of peace and truth" (Est. 9:30), [and truth refers to Torah:] "Buy the truth and do not sell it" (Prov. 23:23).

III. Matters of Philosophy, Natural Science and Metaphysics

This category remains null.

Part Four

LAMENTATIONS RABBATI

25

Lamentations Rabbati Petihtaot

I. The Character of Lamentations Rabbati

The theme of Lamentations Rabbati is Israel's relationship with God, and the message concerning that theme is that the stipulative covenant still and always governs that relationship. Therefore everything that happens to Israel makes sense and bears meaning; and Israel is not helpless before its fate but controls its own destiny. This is the one and whole message of our compilation, and it is the only message that is repeated throughout; everything else proves secondary and derivative of the fundamental proposition that the destruction proves the enduring validity of the covenant, its rules and its promise of redemption.

Lamentations Rabbah's is a covenantal theology, in which Israel and God have mutually and reciprocally agreed to bind themselves to a common Torah; the rules of the relationship are such that an infraction triggers its penalty willy-nilly; but obedience to the Torah likewise brings its reward, in the context envisaged by our compilers, the reward of redemption. The compilation sets forth a single message, which is reworked in only a few ways: Israel suffers because of sin, God will respond to Israel's atonement, on the one side, and loyalty to the covenant in the Torah, on the other. And when Israel has attained the merit that accrues through the Torah, God will redeem Israel. That is the simple, rock-hard and repeated message of this rather protracted reading of the book of Lamentations. Still, Lamentations Rabbah proves nearly as much a commentary in the narrowest sense – verse by verse amplification, paraphrase, exposition – as it is a compilation in the working definition of this inquiry of mine.

What holds the document together and gives it, if not coherence, then at least flow and movement, after all, are the successive passages of (mere) exposition. All the more stunning, therefore, is the simple fact that, when all has been set forth and completed, there really is that simple message that God's unique relationship with Israel, which is unique among the nations, works itself out even now, in a time of despair and disappointment. The resentment of the present condition, recapitulating the calamity of the destruction of the Temple, finds its resolution and remission in the redemption that will follow Israel's regeneration through the Torah – that is the program, that is the proposition, and in this compilation, there is no other.

Logic of Coherent Discourse

Among the established logics, the propositions represented in this compilation are as follows:

	Number	Percent of the Whole
Propositional and Philosophical Discourse	21	18.75%
Themes Worked out by Teleology Expressed in Narrative	18	16%
The Logic of Fixed Association	59	52%
The Cogency of a Fixed Analytical Method	0	0%
No Clear Coherence between or among Successive Units of Completed Discourse	8	7%
Not Relevant to the Issue	6	5%

If we now ask about the operative logics, that is, the first three entries, the result is as follows:

Propositional and Philosophical Discourse	21	21%
Themes Worked out by Teleology Expressed in Narrative	18	18%
The Logic of Fixed Association	59	60%

The paramount logic of our document is that of fixed association. This is not a "commentary" to the book of Lamentations, but the document is laid out so that it appears to be just that.

Topical Program

Israel's relationship with God is treated with special reference to the covenant, the Torah, and the land. By reason of the sins of the Israelites, they have gone into exile with the destruction of the Temple. The founders of the family, Abraham, Isaac, and Jacob, also went into exile. Now they cannot be accused of lacking in religious duties, attention to teachings of the Torah and of prophecy, carrying out the requirements of righteousness (philanthropy) and good deeds, and the like. The people are at fault for their own condition (I:i.1-7). Torah study defines the condition of Israel, for example, "If you have seen [the inhabitants of] towns uprooted from their places in the land of Israel, know that it is because they did not pay the salary of scribes and teachers" (II.i).

So long as Judah and Benjamin were at home, God could take comfort at the loss of the ten tribes; once they went into exile, God began to mourn (II:ii). Israel survived Pharaoh and Sennacherib, but not God's punishment (III:i). After the disaster in Jeremiah's time, Israel emerged from Eden – but could come back. (IV:i). God did not play favorites among the tribes; when any of them sinned, he punished them through exile (VI:i). Israel was punished because of the ravaging of words of Torah and prophecy, righteous men, religious duties and good deeds (VII:i). The land of Israel, the Torah, and the Temple are ravaged, to the shame of Israel (Jer. 9:19-21) (VIII:i). The Israelites practiced idolatry, still more did the pagans; God was neglected by the people and was left solitary, so God responded to the people's actions (X:i). If you had achieved the merit (using the theological language at hand), then you would have enjoyed everything, but since you did not have the merit, you enjoyed nothing (XI:i).

The Israelites did not trust God, so they suffered disaster (XIII.i). The Israelites scorned God and brought dishonor upon God among the nations (XV:i). While God was generous with the Israelites in the wilderness, under severe conditions, he was harsh with them in civilization, under pleasant conditions, because they sinned and angered him (XVI:i). With merit one drinks good water in Jerusalem, without, bad water in the exile of Babylonia; with merit one sings songs and Psalms in Jerusalem, without, dirges and lamentations in Babylonia. At stake is peoples' merit, not God's grace (XIX:i). The contrast is drawn between redemption and disaster, the giving of the Torah and the destruction of the Temple (XX:i). When the Israelites went into exile among the nations of the world, not one of them could produce a word of Torah from his mouth; God punished Israel for its sins (XXI:i). Idolatry was the cause (XXII:i). The destruction of the Temple was possible only because God had already abandoned it (XXIV:ii). When the Temple was destroyed, God was answerable to the patriarchs for what he had done (XXIV:ii). The Presence of God departed from the Temple by stages (XXV:i).

The Holy One punishes Israel only after bringing testimony against them (XXVII:i). The road that led from the salvation of Hezekiah is the one that brought Israel to the disaster brought about by Nebuchadnezzar. Then the Israelite kings believed, but the pagan king did not believe; and God gave the Israelite kings a reward for their faith, through Hezekiah, and to the pagan king, without his believing and without obeying, were handed over Jerusalem and its Temple (XXX:i). Before the Israelites went into exile, the Holy One, blessed be He, called them bad. But when they had gone into exile, he began to sing their praises (XXXI:i). The Israelites were sent into exile only after they had denied the Unique One of the world, the Ten Commandments, circumcision, which had been given to the twentieth generation [Abraham], and the Pentateuch (XXXV:ii, iii). When the Temple was destroyed and Israel went into exile, God mourned in the manner that mortals do (XXXV:iv). The prophetic critique of Israel is mitigated by mercy. There is no proof that just as the Israelites did not go to extremes in sinning, so the measure of justice did not do so. Israel stands in an ambiguous relationship with God, both divorced and not divorced (XXXV:vi, vii).

Before God penalizes, he has already prepared the healing for the penalty; As to all the harsh prophecies that Jeremiah issued against the Israelites, Isaiah first of all anticipated each and pronounced healing for it (XXXVI:ii). The Israelites err for weeping frivolously, "but in the end there will be a real weeping for good cause" (XXXVI:iv, v). The ten tribes went into exile, but the Presence of God did not go into exile. Judah and Benjamin went into exile, but the Presence of God did not go into exile. But when the children went into exile, then the Presence of God went into exile (XXXIX:iii). The great men of Israel turned their faces away when they saw people sinning, and God did the same to them (XL:ii). When the Israelites carry out the will of the Holy One, they add strength to the strength of heaven, and when they do not, they weaken the power of the One above (XL:ii). The exile and the redemption will match (XL:ii). In her affliction, Jerusalem remembered her rebellion against God (XLI:i).

When the gentile nations sin, there is no sequel in punishment, but when the Israelites sin, they also are punished (XLII:i). God considered carefully how to bring the evil upon Israel (XLVIII:i). God suffers with Israel and for Israel (L:i), a minor theme in a massive compilation of stories. By observing their religious duties the Israelites became distinguished before God (LIII:i). With every thing with which the Israelites sinned, they were smitten, and with that same thing they will be comforted. When they sinned with the head, they were smitten at the head, but they were comforted through the head (LVI:i). There is an exact match between Israel's triumph and Israel's downfall. Thus: Just as these were punished through the destruction effected by priest and prophet [the priests and Joshua at Jericho], so these were subject to priest and prophet [Jeremiah]. Just as these were through the ram's horn and shouting, so Israel will be through ram's horn and shouting (LVII:ii).

God's relationship to Israel was complicated by the relationship to Jacob, thus: "Isn't it the fact that the Israelites are angering me only because of the icon of Jacob that is engraved on my throne? Here, take it, it's thrown in your face!" (LVII:ii). God is engaged with Israel's disaster (LIX:ii). The Israelites did not fully explore the limits of the measure of justice, so the measure of justice did not go to extremes against them (LX:i, LXI:i). God's decree against Jerusalem comes from of old (LXIV:i). God forewarned Israel and showed Israel favor, but it did no good (LXIX:i). God did to Israel precisely what he had threatened long ago (LXXIII:i). But God does not rejoice in punishing Israel (the same). The argument between God and Israel is framed in this way. The community of Israel says that they are the only ones who accepted God; God says, I rejected everybody else for you (LXXIX:ii). Israel accepted its suffering as atonement and asked that the suffering expiate the sin (LXXV:i).

God suffers along with Israel, Israel's loyalty will be recognized and appreciated by God, and, in the meantime, the Israelites will find in the Torah the comfort that they require. The nations will be repaid for their actions toward Israel in the interval. Even though the Holy One, blessed be He, is angry with his servants, the righteous, in this world, in the world to come, he has mercy on them (LXXXVI:i). God is good to those that deserve it (LXXXVII:i). God mourns for Israel the way human mourners mourn (LXXXVIII:i). God will never abandon Israel (LXXXIX:i). The Holy Spirit brings about redemption (XCV:i). It is better to be punished by God than favored by a gentile king, thus: "Better was the removing of the ring by Pharaoh [for the sealing of decrees to oppress the Israelites] than the forty years during which Moses prophesied concerning them, because it was through this [oppression] that the redemption came about, while through that [prophesying] the redemption did not come about" (CXXII:i).

The upshot here is that persecution in the end is good for Israel, because it produces repentance more rapidly than prophecy ever did, with the result that the redemption is that much nearer. The enemy will also be punished for its sins, and, further, God's punishment is appropriate and well-placed. People get what they deserve, both Israel and the others. God should protect Israel and not leave them among the nations, but that is not what he has done (CXXIII:i). God blames that generation for its own fate, and the ancestors claim that the only reason the Israelites endure is because of the merit of the ancestors (CXXIX:i). The redemption of the past tells us about the redemption in the future

(CXXX:i). "The earlier generations, because they smelled the stench of only part of the tribulations inflicted by the idolatrous kingdoms, became impatient. But we, who dwell in the midst of the four kingdoms, how much the more so [are we impatient]!" (CXXXI:i).

God's redemption is certain, so people who are suffering should be glad, since that is a guarantee of coming redemption, thus "For if those who outrage him he treats in such a way, those who do his will all the more so!" So if the words of Uriah are carried out, the words of Zechariah will be carried out, while if the words of Uriah prove false, then the words of Zechariah will not be true either. "I was laughing with pleasure because the words of Uriah have been carried out, and that means that the words of Zechariah in the future will be carried out" (CXL:i). The Temple will be restored, and Israel will regain its place, as God's throne and consort, respectively (CXLI:i). Punishment and rejection will be followed by forgiveness and reconciliation (CXLII:i). The Jews can accomplish part of the task on their own, even though they throw themselves wholly on God's mercy. The desired age is either like that of Adam, or like that of Moses and Solomon, or like that of Noah and Abel; all three possibilities link the coming redemption to a time of perfection, Eden, or the age prior to idolatry, or the time of Moses and Solomon, the builders of the cult and the Temple, respectively (CXLIII:i). If there is rejection, then there is no hope, but if there is anger, there is hope, because someone who is angry may in the end be appeased. Whenever there is an allusion to divine anger, that, too, is a mark of hope (CXLIV:i).

Israel's relationship with the nations is treated with interest in Israel's history, past, present, and future, and how that cyclical is to be known. But there is no theory of "the other," or the outsider here; the nations are the enemy; the compilers find nothing of merit to report about them. Israel's difference from the other, for which God is responsible, accounts for the dislike that the nations express toward Israel; Israel's present condition as minority, different and despised on account of the difference, is God's fault and choice. Israel was besieged not only by the Babylonians but also the neighbors, the Ammonites and Moabites (IX:i), and God will punish them, too. The public ridicule of Jews' religious rites contrasts with the Jews' own perception of their condition. The exposition of Ps. 69:13 in terms of gentiles' ridicule of Jews' practices – the Jews' poverty, their Sabbath and Seventh Year observance – is followed by a re-exposition of the Jews' practices, now with respect to the ninth of Ab (XVII:i). Even though the nations of the world go into exile, their exile is not really an exile at all. But as for Israel, their exile really is an exile. The nations of the world, who eat the bread and drink the wine of others, do not really experience exile. But the Israelites, who do not eat the bread and drink the wine of others, really do experience exile (XXXVII:i).

The Ammonites and Moabites joined with the enemy and behaved very spitefully (XLIV:i). When the Israelites fled from the destruction of Jerusalem, the nations of the world sent word everywhere to which they fled and shut them out (LV:i). But this was to be blamed on God: "If we had intermarried with them, they would have accepted us" (LXIX:i). There are ten references to "might" of Israel; when the Israelites sinned, these forms of might were taken away from them and given to the nations of the world. The nations of the world ridicule the Jews for their religious observances (LXXXIII:i). These propositions simply expose, in their own framework, the same proposition as the ones concerning God's relationship to Israel and Israel's relationship to God. The relationship between Israel and the nations forms a subset of the relationship of Israel and God; nothing in the former relationship happens on its own, but all things express in this mundane context the rules and effects of the rules that govern in the transcendent one. All we learn about Israel and the nations is that the covenant endures, bearing its own inevitable sanctions and consequences.

Our authorship has little interest in Israel out of relationship with either God or the nations. Israel on its own forms a subordinated and trivial theme; whatever messages we do find take on meaning only in the initial framework, that defined by Israel's relationship with God. Israel is never on its own. The bitterness of the ninth of Ab is contrasted with the bitter herbs with which the first redemption is celebrated (XVIII:i). The same contrast is drawn between the giving of the Torah and the destruction of the Temple (XX:i). If Israel had found rest among the nations, she would not have returned to the holy land (XXXVII:ii). The glory of Israel lay in its relationship to God, in the sanhedrin, in the disciples of sages, in the priestly watches, in the children (XL:i). Israel first suffers, then rejoices; her unfortunate condition marks the fact that Israel stands at the center of things (LIX:iii). Israel has declined through the generations, thus: "In olden times, when people held the sanhedrin in awe, naughty words were never included in songs. But when the sanhedrin was abolished, naughty words were inserted in songs. In olden times, when troubles came upon Israel, they stopped rejoicing on that account. Now that both have come to an end [no more singing, no more banquet halls], 'The joy of our hearts has ceased; our dancing has been turned to mourning'" (CXXXVII:i). None of this bears any interesting message.

II. Unarticulated Premises: The Givens of Religious Conduct

No halakhic matters demand attention.

III. Unarticulated Premises: The Givens of Religious Conviction

1. Calamities overtake Israel because of neglect of the Torah; so long as Israel studies the Torah and carries out its teachings, its future is secure. This theme is dominant in the document, and I do not catalogue every instance in which the premise of discussion goes over the present point.

II

I.10 A. Said R. Abba bar Kahana, "There arose among the nations no philosophers like Balaam b. Beor and Oeonamos of Gadara.

    B. "They said to them, 'Can we vanquish this nation?'

    C. "They said to them, 'Go and make the rounds of their synagogues and schoolhouses. If children are chirping in loud voices, you cannot overcome them, but if not, you can overcome them.

    D. "'For so did their Father promise them, saying to them, "The voice is the voice of Jacob, but the hands are the hands of Esau" (Gen. 27:22).

    E. "'So long as the voice of Jacob chirps in the synagogues and schoolhouses, the hands are not the hands of Esau, and when his voice does not chirp in the synagogues and schoolhouses, the hands are the hands of Esau.'

    F. "And so Scripture says, 'Therefore as stubble devours the tongue of fire' (Isa. 5:24).

    G. "Now does stubble consume fire? But is it not the way of fire to consume stubble?

    H. "So can you say, 'Therefore as stubble devours the tongue of fire' (Isa. 5:24)?

    I. "But 'stubble' refers to the house of Esau, as it is said, 'And the house of Jacob shall be a fire, and the house of Joseph a flame, and the house of Esau stubble' (Obad. 18).

    J. "'the tongue of fire' ['as stubble devours the tongue of fire' (Isa. 5:24)] refers to the house of Jacob, which is compared to fire: 'And the house of Jacob shall be a fire.'

    K. "'And as the chaff is consumed in the flame' speaks of the house of Joseph, compared to flame: 'and the house of Joseph a flame.'

    L. "'So their root shall be as rottenness' (Isa. 5:24): this refers to the patriarchs, who are Israelite's root.

    M. "'And their blossom shall go up as dust' speaks of the tribes, who are Israel's blossoms.

    N. "On what account?

    O. "'Because they rejected the Torah of the Lord of hosts [and condemned the word of the Holy One of Israel' (Obad. 18)."

I.11 A. Said R. Yudan, "'Because they rejected the Torah of the Lord of hosts':

    B. "this refers to the Written Torah.

C.   "'and condemned the word of the Holy One of Israel' (Obad. 18):

D.   "this refers to the memorized Torah."

2.   Israel's history in the land is the counterpart of Adam's history in Eden; with the destruction of Jerusalem in 586, Israel was driven out of Eden. But Israel can come back.

IV

I.1   A.   R. Abbahu in the name of R. Yosé bar Haninah commenced [discourse by citing this verse]: "'But they are like a man, they have transgressed the covenant. There they dealt treacherously against me' (Hos. 6:7).

        B.   "'They are like a man,' specifically, this refers to the first man [Adam]. [We shall now compare the story of the first man in Eden with the story of Israel in its land.]

        C.   "Said the Holy One, blessed be He, 'In the case of the first man, I brought him into the garden of Eden, I commanded him, he violated my commandment, I judged him to be sent away and driven out, but I mourned for him, saying "How..."' [which begins the book of Lamentations, hence stands for a lament, but which also is written with the consonants that also yield, 'Where are you'].

        D.   "'I brought him into the garden of Eden,' as it is written, 'And the Lord God took the man and put him into the garden of Eden' (Gen. 2:15).

        E.   "'I commanded him,' as it is written, 'And the Lord God commanded...' (Gen. 2:16).

        F.   "'And he violated my commandment,' as it is written, 'Did you eat from the tree concerning which I commanded you' (Gen. 3:11).

        G.   "'I judged him to be sent away,' as it is written, 'And the Lord God sent him from the garden of Eden' (Gen. 3:23).

        H.   "'And I judged him to be driven out.' 'And he drove out the man' (Gen. 3:24).

        I.   "'But I mourned for him, saying, How.... 'And He said to him, Where are you' (Gen. 3:9), and the word for 'where are you' is written, 'How....'

        J.   "'So, too, in the case of his descendants, [God continues to speak,] I brought them into the Land of Israel, I commanded them, they violated my commandment, I judged them to be sent out and driven away but I mourned for them, saying, "How...."'

        K.   "'I brought them into the Land of Israel': 'And I brought you into the land of Carmel' (Jer. 2:7).

        L.   "'I commanded them': 'And you, command the children of Israel' (Ex. 27:20). 'Command the children of Israel' (Lev. 24:2).

        M.   "'They violated my commandment': 'And all Israel have violated your Torah' (Dan. 9:11).

        N.   "'I judged them to be sent out': 'Send them away, out of my sight and let them go forth' (Jer. 15:1).

        O.   "'....and driven away': 'From my house I shall drive them' (Hos. 9:15).

        P.   "'But I mourned for them, saying, How...': 'How lonely sits the city [that was full of people! How like a widow has she become, she

that was great among the nations! She that was a princess among
the cities has become a vassal. She weeps bitterly in the night, tears
on her cheeks, among all her lovers she has none to comfort her; all
her friends have dealt treacherously with her, they have become her
enemies]' (Lam. 1:1-2)."

3.   Merit [zekhut] governs Israel's destiny:

<h1 style="text-align:center">XI</h1>

I.1   A.   R. Isaac commenced [by citing the following verse of Scripture]:
             "'Because you would not serve the Lord your God in joy and
             gladness over the abundance of everything, you shall have to serve
             in hunger and thirst, naked and lacking everything, the enemies
             whom the Lord will let loose against you. He will put an iron yoke
             upon your neck until he has wiped you out' (Deut. 28:47-48).

       B.   "Had you had the merit, you would have read in the Torah: 'You
             will bring them in and plant them in the mountain of your
             inheritance' (Ex. 15:17).

       C.   "But since you did not have the merit: 'Let all their wickedness
             come before you' (Lam. 1:22).

       D.   "Had you had the merit, you would have read in the Torah: 'The
             peoples have heard, they tremble' (Ex. 15:14).

       E.   "But since you did not have the merit: 'They have heard that I sigh'
             (Lam. 1:21).

       F.   "Had you had the merit, you would have read in the Torah: 'I have
             surely seen the affliction of my people that are in Egypt' (Ex. 3:7).

       G.   "But since you did not have the merit: 'O Lord, for I am in distress,
             mine innards burn' (Lam. 1:20).

       H.   "Had you had the merit, you would have read in the Torah: 'And
             you shall make proclamation on the selfsame day' (Lev. 23:21).

       I.   "But since you did not have the merit: 'I called for my lovers but
             they deceived me' (Lam. 1:19).

       J.   "Had you had the merit, you would have read in the Torah: 'Justice,
             justice you shall follow' (Deut. 16:20).

       K.   "But since you did not have the merit: 'The Lord is just, for I have
             rebelled against his word' (Lam. 1:18).

       L.   "Had you had the merit, you would have read in the Torah: 'You
             shall surely open your hand to your brother' (Deut. 15:11).

       M.   "But since you did not have the merit: 'Zion spreads forth her
             hands' (Lam. 1:17).

       N.   "Had you had the merit, you would have read in the Torah: 'These
             are the appointed seasons of the Lord' (Lev. 23:4).

       O.   "But since you did not have the merit: 'These things I weep' (Lam.
             1:16).

       P.   "Had you had the merit, you would have read in the Torah: 'We
             will go up by the highway' (Num. 20:19).

       Q.   "But since you did not have the merit: 'The Lord has set at nought
             all my mighty men' [the word play is on highway, "messilah," and
             nought, "sillah"].

       R.   "Had you had the merit, you would have read in the Torah: 'And I
             have broken the bars of your yoke' (Lev. 26:13).

S.   "But since you did not have the merit: 'The yoke of my transgressions is impressed by his hand' (Lam. 1:14).

T.   "Had you had the merit, you would have read in the Torah: 'Fire shall be kept burning upon the altar continually' (Lev. 6:6).

U.   "But since you did not have the merit: 'From on high he has sent fire into my bones' (Lam. 1:13).

V.   "Had you had the merit, you would have read in the Torah: 'In all the way that you went' (Deut. 1:31).

W.   "But since you did not have the merit: 'Let it not come to you, all you that pass in the way' (Lam. 1:12).

X.   "Had you had the merit, you would have read in the Torah: 'And you shall eat your bread until you have enough' (Lev. 26:5).

Y.   "But since you did not have the merit: 'All her people sigh, they seek bread' (Lam. 1:11).

Z.   "Had you had the merit, you would have read in the Torah: 'Neither shall any man covet your land' (Ex. 34:24).

AA.   "But since you did not have the merit: 'The enemy has spread out his hand upon all her coveted treasures' (Lam. 1:10).

BB.   "Had you had the merit, you would have read in the Torah: 'For on this day shall atonement be made for you to cleanse you' (Lev. 16:30).

CC.   "But since you did not have the merit: 'Her filthiness was in her skirts' (Lam. 1:9).

DD.   "Had you had the merit, you would have read in the Torah: 'From all your sins shall you be clean before the Lord' (Lev. 16:30).

EE.   "But since you did not have the merit: 'Jerusalem has grievously sinned' (Lam. 1:8).

FF.   "Had you had the merit, you would have read in the Torah: 'And you shall be remembered before the Lord your God' (Num. 10:9).

GG.   "But since you did not have the merit: 'Jerusalem remembers in the days of her afflictions' (Lam. 1:7).

HH.   "Had you had the merit, you would have read in the Torah: 'And I will walk among you' (Lev. 26:12).

II.   "But since you did not have the merit: 'And gone is from the daughter of Zion all her splendor' (Lam. 1:6).

JJ.   "Had you had the merit, you would have read in the Torah: 'And the Lord will make you the head' (Deut. 28:13).

KK.   "But since you did not have the merit: 'Her adversaries are become the head, her enemies are at ease' (Lam. 1:5).

LL.   "Had you had the merit, you would have read in the Torah: 'Three times a year shall all your males appear before the Lord' (Deut. 16:16).

MM.   "But since you did not have the merit: 'The ways of Zion do mourn' (Lam. 1:4).

NN.   "Had you had the merit, you would have read in the Torah: 'And you shall dwell in your land safely' (Lev. 26:5).

OO.   "But since you did not have the merit: 'Judah has gone into exile because of affliction' (Lam. 1:3).

PP.   "Had you had the merit, you would have read in the Torah: 'It was a night of watching unto the Lord' (Ex. 12:42).

QQ. "But since you did not have the merit: 'She weeps sore in the night' (Lam. 1:2).

RR. "Had you had the merit, you would have read in the Torah: 'How can I myself bear' (Deut. 1:12).

SS. "But since you did not have the merit: 'How lonely sits the city once great with people!' (Lam. 1:1)."

IV. Matters of Philosophy, Natural Science and Metaphysics

Nothing comes under consideration.

26

Lamentations Rabbati Parashah One

I. Unarticulated Premises: The Givens of Religious Conduct

The category is inert.

II. Unarticulated Premises: The Givens of Religious Conviction

1. God was affected by, and mourned for, the destruction of Jerusalem:

XXXV

IV.1 A. Another matter concerning "[How] lonely sits [the city that was full of people]" [now with stress on "sits," in its sense of "sitting in mourning":]

B. Said R. Nahman, "The Holy One, blessed be He, asked the ministering angels, 'A mortal king in mourning – what is fitting for him to do?'

C. "They said to him, 'He hangs sacking on his door.'

D. "He said to them, 'I, too, will do so': 'I clothe the heavens with blackness, and I make sackcloth their covering' (Isa. 50:3).

E. "'What else does a mortal king do?'

F. "'He turns down the lamps.'

G. "'I, too, will do so': 'The sun and the moon are become black, the stars withdraw their shining' (Joel 4:15).

H. "'What else?'

I. "'He turns over the couch.'

J. "'I, too': 'Until thrones were cast down, and One that was ancient of days did sit' (Dan. 7:9).

K. "It is as though they were overturned [in mourning].

L. "'What else?'

M. "'He goes barefoot.'

N. "'I, too': 'The Lord in the whirlwind and in the storm is his way, and clouds are the dust of his feet' (Nah. 1:5).

O. "'What else?'

P. "'He tears his purple clothing.'

Q.   "'I, too': 'The Lord has done that which he devised, he has performed his word' (Lam. 2:17)."

R.   What is the meaning of "that which he devised"?

S.   R. Jacob of Kefar Hanan said, "He tore his purple."

T.   [Continuing from Q:] "'What else?'

U.   "'He sits in silence.'

V.   "'I, too': 'He sits alone and keeps silent' (Lam. 3:28).

W.   "'What else?'

X.   "'He sits and weeps.'

Y.   "'I, too': 'How lonely sits....'"

2.   Israel's special observances make its exile more painful than exile affecting gentiles:

XXXVII

I.1   A.   "Judah has gone into exile":

B.   Do not the nations of the world go into exile?

C.   Even though they go into exile, their exile is not really an exile at all.

D.   But for Israel, their exile really is an exile.

E.   The nations of the world, who eat the bread and drink the wine of others, do not really experience exile.

F.   But the Israelites, who do not eat the bread and drink the wine of others, really do experience exile.

G.   The nations of the world, who [Cohen, p. 96:] travel in litters, do not really experience exile.

H.   But the Israelites, who [in poverty] go barefoot – their exile really is an exile.

I.   That is why it is said, "Judah has gone into exile."

3.   God carefully planned the punishment of Israel, so that it would be tolerable, and this was in both political and human terms:

XLVIII

I.1   A.   "My transgressions were bound into a yoke; by his hand they were fastened together":

B.   [Following Cohen on the word "were bound,"] "I was mistaken with regard to my iniquities.

C.   "I thought that he would forgive me them all, when I heard that my indictment had been read on high."

I.2   A.   Another interpretation of the word for "bound" in the verse, "My transgressions were bound into a yoke; by his hand they were fastened together":

B.   Reading the word as though it were written to mean "consider carefully,"

C.   he considered carefully how to bring evil upon me.

D.   He thought, "If I send them into exile in the winter season, there will be no grapes on the vine or figs on the fig trees. I will send them into exile in the summer season, when there are grapes on the vine and figs on the fig trees, so that they will easily find food and drink on the way."

I.3 A. Another interpretation of the word for "bound" in the verse, "My transgressions were bound into a yoke; by his hand they were fastened together":

  B. Reading the word as though it were written to mean "consider carefully,"

  C. he considered carefully how to bring evil upon me.

  D. He thought, "If I send them into exile in the winter season, lo, all of them will die from cold. I shall send them into exile in the summer season, so that even if they sleep in the marketplaces or on the roads, they will not be injured."

I.4 A. Another interpretation of the word for "bound" in the verse, "My transgressions were bound into a yoke; by his hand they were fastened together":

  B. Reading the word as though it were written to mean "consider carefully,"

  C. he considered carefully how to bring evil upon me.

  D. He thought, "If I send them into exile in the wilderness, they will die of hunger. I shall send them into exile by way of Armenia, where there are towns and cities, so that they can find food and drink."

I.5 A. "My transgressions were bound into a yoke; by his hand they were fastened together":

  B. [Following Cohen on the word "were bound,"] "I was mistaken with regard to my iniquities.

  C. "I thought that he would forgive me them all, but 'they were set upon my neck.'"

I.6 A. ["They were set upon my neck," reading the word "set" to mean,] "knit together":

  B. He brought them against me at intervals.

  C. He brought them upon me in pairs: Babylon and the Chaldeans, Media and Persia, Greece and Macedon, Edom and Ishmael.

  D. He alternated them as to their behavior: Babylon was harsh, Media lenient, Greece harsh, Edom lenient, the Chaldeans harsh, Persia lenient, Macedon harsh, Ishmael lenient:

  E. "So part of the kingdom shall be strong, and part broken" (Dan. 2:42).

4. God's punishment is very exact, the penalty fitting the crime with great precision, but that also brings assurance that the redemption that is coming will bring comfort in due proportion as well:

LVI

I.2 A. "For my groans are many and my heart is faint":

  B. You find that with every thing with which the Israelites sinned, they were smitten, and with that same thing they will be comforted. When they sinned with the head, they were smitten at the head, but they were comforted through the head.

  C. "When they sinned with the head": "Let us make a head and let us return to Egypt" (Num. 14:4).

  D. "...they were smitten at the head": "The whole head is sick" (Isa. 1:5).

| | E. | "...but they were comforted through the head": "Their king has passed before them and the Lord is at the head of them" (Mic. 2:13). |

I.3   A.   When they sinned with the eye, they were smitten at the eye, but they were comforted through the eye.

B.   "When they sinned with the eye": "[The daughters of Zion...walk]...with wanton eyes" (Isa. 3:16).

C.   "...they were smitten at the eye": "My eye, my eye runs down with water" (Lam. 1:16).

D.   "...but they were comforted through the eye": "For every eye shall see the Lord returning to Zion" (Isa. 52:8).

I.4   A.   When they sinned with the ear, they were smitten at the ear, but they were comforted through the ear.

B.   "When they sinned with the ear": "They stopped up their ears so as not to hear" (Zech. 7:11).

C.   "...they were smitten at the ear": "Their ears shall be deaf" (Mic. 7:16).

D.   "...but they were comforted through the ear": "Your ears shall hear a word saying, [This is the way]" (Isa. 30:21).

I.5   A.   When they sinned with the nose [spelled af, which can also mean, "yet" or "also"] they were smitten at the nose, but they were comforted through the nose.

B.   "When they sinned with the nose": "And lo, they put the branch to their noses" (Ezek. 8:17).

C.   "...they were smitten at the word af [also]": "I also will do this to you" (Lev. 26:16).

D.   "...but they were comforted through the word af [now meaning yet]": "And yet for all that, when they are in the land of their enemies, I will not reject them" (Lev. 26:44).

I.6   A.   When they sinned with the mouth, they were smitten at the mouth, but they were comforted through the mouth.

B.   "When they sinned with the mouth": "Every mouth speaks wantonness" (Isa. 9:16).

C.   "...they were smitten at the mouth": "[The Aramaeans and the Philistines] devour Israel with open mouth" (Isa. 9:11).

D.   "...but they were comforted through the mouth": "Then was our mouth filled with laughter" (Ps. 126:2).

I.7   A.   When they sinned with the tongue, they were smitten at the tongue, but they were comforted through the tongue.

B.   "When they sinned with the tongue": "They bend their tongue, [their bow of falsehood]" (Jer. 9:2).

C.   "...they were smitten at the tongue": "The tongue of the sucking [child cleaves to the roof of his mouth for thirst]" (Lam. 4:4).

D.   "...but they were comforted through the tongue": "And our tongue with singing" (Ps. 126:2).

I.8   A.   When they sinned with the heart, they were smitten at the heart, but they were comforted through the heart.

B.   "When they sinned with the heart": "Yes, they made their hearts as a stubborn stone" (Zech. 7:12).

C.   "...they were smitten at the heart": "And the whole heart faints" (Isa. 1:5).

	D.	"...but they were comforted through the heart": "Speak to the heart of Jerusalem" (Isa. 40:2).
I.9	A.	When they sinned with the hand, they were smitten at the hand, but they were comforted through the hand.
	B.	"When they sinned with the hand": "Your hands are full of blood" (Isa. 1:15).
	C.	"...they were smitten at the hand": "The hands of women full of compassion have boiled their own children" (Lam. 4:10).
	D.	"...but they were comforted through the hand": "The Lord will set his hand again the second time [to recover the remnant of his people]" (Isa. 11:11).
I.10	A.	When they sinned with the foot, they were smitten at the foot, but they were comforted through the foot.
	B.	"When they sinned with the foot": "The daughters of Zion...walk...making a tinkling with their feet" (Isa. 3:16).
	C.	"...they were smitten at the foot": "Your feet will stumble upon the dark mountains" (Jer. 13:16).
	D.	"...but they were comforted through the foot": "How beautiful upon the mountains are the feet of the messenger of good tidings" (Isa. 52:7).
I.11	A.	When they sinned with this, they were smitten at this, but they were comforted through this.
	B.	"When they sinned with this": "[The people said...Go, make us a god], for as for this man Moses..., [we do not know what has become of him]" (Ex. 32:1).
	C.	"...they were smitten at this": "For this our heart is faint" (Lam. 5:17).
	D.	"...but they were comforted through this": "It shall be said in that day, Lo, this is our God" (Isa. 25:9).
I.12	A.	When they sinned with he, they were smitten at he, but they were comforted through he.
	B.	"When they sinned with he": "They have denied the Lord and said, It is not he" (Jer. 5:12).
	C.	"...they were smitten at he": "Therefore he has turned to be their enemy, and he himself fought against them" (Isa. 63:10).
	D.	"...but they were comforted through he": "I even I am he who comforts you" (Isa. 51:12).
I.13	A.	When they sinned with fire, they were smitten at fire, but they were comforted through fire.
	B.	"When they sinned with fire": "The children gather wood and the fathers kindle fire" (Jer. 7:18).
	C.	"...they were smitten at fire": "For from on high he has sent fire into my bones" (Lam. 1:13).
	D.	"...but they were comforted through fire": "For I, says the Lord, will be for her a wall of fire round about" (Zech. 2:9).
I.14	A.	When they sinned in double measure, they were smitten in double measure, but they were comforted in double measure.
	B.	"When they sinned in double measure": "Jerusalem has sinned a sin" (Lam. 1:8).
	C.	"...they were smitten in double measure": "that she has received from the Lord's hand double for all her sins" (Isa. 40:2).

D.   "...but they were comforted in double measure": "Comfort, comfort
      my people, says your God. [Speak tenderly to the heart of Jerusalem
      and cry to her that her warfare is ended, that her iniquity is
      pardoned, that she has received from the Lord's hand double for all
      her sins]" (Isa. 40:1-2).

III. Matters of Philosophy, Natural Science and Metaphysics

Nothing pertains.

27

Lamentations Rabbati Parashah Two

I. Unarticulated Premises: The Givens of Religious Conduct

I see no candidates for inclusion.

II. Unarticulated Premises: The Givens of Religious Conviction

1. Arrogance against heaven accounts for Israel's defeat, as in the case of Bar Kokhba:

LVIII

II.8   A.   When they went out to battle, he would say, "Lord of all ages, don't help us and don't hinder us!"

        B.   That is in line with this verse: "Have you not, O God, cast us off? And do not go forth, O God, with our hosts" (Ps. 60:12).

III. Matters of Philosophy, Natural Science and Metaphysics

Nothing belongs here.

28

Lamentations Rabbati Parashah Three

I. Unarticulated Premises: The Givens of Religious Conduct

There is nothing of halakhic interest here.

II. Unarticulated Premises: The Givens of Religious Conviction

1. God's faithfulness endures, and evidence of that fact is the very condition of Israel among the nations:

LXXXVI

I.1   A.   "The steadfast love of the Lord never ceases, his mercies never come to an end":

         B.   Said R. Simeon b. Laqish, "Even though the Holy One, blessed be He, is angry with his servants, the righteous, in this world, in the world to come, he has mercy on them.

         C.   "That is in line with this verse: 'The steadfast love of the Lord never ceases, his mercies never come to an end.'"

I.2   A.   "They are new every morning; great is your faithfulness":

         B.   Said R. Alexandri, "Because you renew us every morning, we know that 'great is your faithfulness.'"

         C.   R. Simon bar Abba said, "Because you renew us in the morning of the nations, we know that 'great is your faithfulness' to redeem us."

III. Matters of Philosophy, Natural Science and Metaphysics

The category does not fit the data.

29

Lamentations Rabbati Parashah Four

I. Unarticulated Premises: The Givens of Religious Conduct

The laws are to be inferred from the actions of sages, as much as from the Mishnah's or Scripture's explicit formulations:

CXX

I.1   A.   "The breath of our nostrils, the Lord's anointed, was taken in their pits, he of whom we said, 'Under his shadow we shall live among the nations'":

       B.   Rabbi [Judah the Patriarch] and R. Ishmael b. R. Yosé were explaining passages of the scroll of Lamentations on the eve of the ninth of Ab that coincided with a Saturday. They omitted one go-around of the alphabet [that is, a chapter], saying, "Tomorrow we'll come back and finish it."

       C.   When Rabbi went home, he had an accident that injured his finger, and recited in his own regard the following verse of Scripture: "Many are the sorrows of the wicked" (Ps. 32:10).

       D.   Said to him R. Ishmael b. R. Yosé, "Were we not engaged in the matter and such a thing had happened to you, I all the more so would have said what I shall now say: "The breath of our nostrils, the Lord's anointed, was taken in their pits, he of whom we said, 'Under his shadow we shall live among the nations.'"

       E.   When they went into his house, he put on it a dry sponge and tied it around the outside with reed grass.

       F.   R. Ishmael b. R. Yosé said, "From that action of his we have derived three things [concerning conduct on the Sabbath day]: [1] a dry sponge may be used on the Sabbath not because it can heal the wound but because it guards the wound; [2] reed grass inside the house is deemed made ready in advance of the Sabbath for use on the Sabbath [and hence permissible; by contrast, objects not designated in advance of the holy day for use on that day may not be used]; [3] people may recite Scripture [on the Sabbath] only after the afternoon prayer, but they may study and expound them."

II. Unarticulated Premises: The Givens of Religious Conviction

I find nothing fresh.

III. Matters of Philosophy, Natural Science and Metaphysics

This rubric remains useless.

30

Lamentations Rabbati Parashah Five

I. Unarticulated Premises: The Givens of Religious Conduct

I find nothing of halakhic interest.

II. Unarticulated Premises: The Givens of Religious Conviction

1. The nations' prosperity now is a sign of the certainty of Israel's redemption in time to come:

CXL

I.1　A.　"For Mount Zion which lies desolate; jackals prowl over it":

　　B.　Rabban Gamaliel, R. Joshua, R. Eleazar b. Azariah, and R. Aqiba went to Rome. They heard the din of the city of Rome from a distance of a hundred and twenty miles.

　　C.　They all began to cry, but R. Aqiba began to laugh.

　　D.　They said to him, "Aqiba, we are crying and you laugh?"

　　E.　He said to them, "Why are you crying?"

　　F.　They said to him, "Should we not cry, that idolators and those who sacrifice to idols and bow down to images live securely and prosperously, while the footstool of our God has been burned down by fire and become a dwelling place for the beasts of the field? So shouldn't we cry?"

　　G.　He said to them, "That is precisely the reason that I was laughing. For if those who outrage him he treats in such a way, those who do his will all the more so!"

I.2　A.　There was the further case of when they were going up to Jerusalem. When they came to the Mount of Olives they tore their clothing. When they came to the Temple mount and a fox came out of the house of the Holy of Holies, they began to cry. But R. Aqiba began to laugh.

　　B.　"Aqiba, you are always surprising us. Now we are crying and you laugh?"

　　C.　He said to them, "Why are you crying?"

D.   They said to him, "Should we not cry, that from the place of which it is written, 'And the ordinary person that comes near shall be put to death' (Num. 1:51) a fox comes out? So the verse of Scripture is carried out: 'for Mount Zion which lies desolate; jackals prowl over it.'"

E.   He said to them, "That is precisely the reason that I was laughing. For Scripture says, 'And I will take for myself faithful witnesses to record, Uriah the priest and Zechariah the son of Jeberechiah' (Isa. 8:2).

F.   "Now what is the relationship between Uriah and Zechariah? Uriah lived in the time of the first temple, Zechariah in the time of the second!

G.   "But Uriah said, 'Thus says the Lord of hosts: Zion shall be plowed as a field, and Jerusalem shall become heaps' (Jer. 26:18).

H.   "And Zechariah said, 'There shall yet be old men and old women sitting in the piazzas of Jerusalem, every man with his staff in his hand for old age' (Zech. 8:4).

I.   "And further: 'And the piazzas of the city shall be full of boys and girls playing in the piazzas thereof' (Zech. 8:5).

J.   "Said the Holy One, blessed be He, 'Now lo, I have these two witnesses. So if the words of Uriah are carried out, the words of Zechariah will be carried out, while if the words of Uriah prove false, then the words of Zechariah will not be true either.'

K.   "I was laughing with pleasure because the words of Uriah have been carried out, and that means that the words of Zechariah in the future will be carried out."

L.   They said to him, "Aqiba, you have given us consolation. May you be comforted among those who are comforted."

III. Matters of Philosophy, Natural Science and Metaphysics

The rubric covers nothing of this parashah.

Part Five

THE FATHERS ACCORDING TO
RABBI NATHAN

31

The Fathers According to
Rabbi Nathan Chapter One

I. The Character of The Fathers According to Rabbi Nathan

In 250, Mishnah-tractate Avot, The Fathers, delivered its message through aphorisms assigned to named sages. A few centuries later – the date is indeterminate but it is possibly ca. 500 – The Fathers According to Rabbi Nathan, a vast secondary expansion of that same tractate, endowed those anonymous names with flesh-and-blood form, recasting the tractate by adding a sizable number of narratives. The authorship of the Mishnah tractate, The Fathers, ca. 250, presented its teachings in the form of aphorisms, rarely finding it necessary to supply those aphorisms with a narrative setting, and never resorting to narrative for the presentation of its propositions. The testamentary authorship, The Fathers According to Rabbi Nathan, provided a vast amplification and supplement to The Fathers and introduced into its treatment of the received tractate a vast corpus of narratives of various sorts. In this way, the later authorship indicated that it found in narrative in general, and stories about sages in particular, modes of discourse for presenting its message that the earlier authorship did not utilize. And the choice of the medium bore implicit meanings, also, for the message that would emerge in the later restatement of the received tractate.

To call The Fathers According to Rabbi Nathan the talmud (or the tosefta) of The Fathers leads to the false expectation that the successor document subjects the principal one to sustained analytical reading. But the character of The Fathers does not sustain analysis, since the compilation presents no theses for argumentation, only wise sayings. The work of The Fathers according to Rabbi Nathan was defined by the fact that the authorship of The Fathers presented the message of sages solely in aphoristic form. Apophthegms bore the entire weight of that authorship's propositions, and – quite consistently – what made one saying cogent with others fore and aft was solely the position of the authority behind that saying: here, not there.

Among the four types of narrative (in a moment defined in detail in our treatment of the teleological logic of coherent discourse that prevails) we find in The Fathers According to Rabbi Nathan, precedent, precipitant, parable, and story (whether an expansion of one that was scriptural or one that concerned sages), three have no counterpart in The Fathers, and therein lies the definition, as a talmud, of The Fathers According to Rabbi Nathan. The authorship of the Fathers completely neglected three. The authorship of The Fathers fully acknowledged the importance of the past, referring to historical events of Scripture. But they did not retell and include in their composition the scriptural stories of what had happened long ago. They understood that their predecessors lived exemplary lives. But they did not narrate stories about sages. They had every reason to appreciate the power of parable. But they did not think it necessary to harness that power for delivering their particular message, or even for stating in colorful ways the propositions they wished to impart. The framers of The Fathers resorted to narrative, but only to serve as a precipitant, with great economy to describe the setting in which a stunning saying was set forth. They did not cite narratives in the form of precedents.

Given a saying of an apophthegmatic character, whether or not that saying is drawn from The Fathers, the authorship of the Fathers According to Rabbi Nathan will do one of the following:

[1]   give a secondary expansion, including an exemplification, of the wise saying at hand;

[2]   cite a prooftext of Scripture in that same connection;

[3]   provide a parable to illustrate the wise saying (as often as not instead of the prooftext).

These three exercises in the structuring of their document – selecting materials and organizing them in a systematic way – the authors of The Fathers According to Rabbi Nathan learned from the framers of The Fathers. In addition they contributed two further principles of structuring their document:

[4]   add a sizable composition of materials that intersect with the foregoing, either by amplifying on the prooftext without regard to the wise saying served by the prooftext, or by enriching discourse on a topic introduced in connection with the base saying;

[5]   tack on a protracted story of a sage and what he said and did, which story may or may not exemplify the teaching of the apophthegm at hand.

The Fathers According to Rabbi Nathan presents two types of materials and sets them forth in a fixed order. The document contains [1] amplifications of sayings in The Fathers as well as [2] materials not related to anything in the original document. The order in which The Fathers According to Rabbi Nathan arranges its types of material becomes immediately clear.   First, that authorship presents amplifications of the prior document, and, only second, does it tack on its own message. The Fathers According to Rabbi Nathan first of all presents itself as continuous with the prior document, and then shows itself to be connected to it. That of course is the strategy of both Talmuds in connecting on the Mishnah. And, of course, where the authorship gives us compositions that are essentially new both in rhetoric and in logic and in topic, it is in that second set of materials that we find what is fresh. Let me spell out matters as they will soon become clear. Where the authorship of the later document has chosen [1] to cite and amplify sayings in the earlier one, that exercise comes first. There may be additional amplification, and what appears to augment often turns out to be quite new and to enter the second of our two categories, in the form of [i] prooftexts drawn from Scripture, or [ii] parables, [iii] other sorts of stories, sometimes involving named sages, that illustrate the same point, and [iv] sequences of unadorned sayings, not in The Fathers, that make the same point. These come later in a sequence of discourses in The Fathers According to Rabbi Nathan. Where an appendix of secondary materials on a theme introduced in the primary discourse occurs, it will be inserted directly after the point at which said theme is located in the counterpart, in the later document, to that passage in the earlier one, and only afterward will the exposition of the saying in The Fathers proceed to a further point. This general order predominates throughout.

The authorship of The Fathers According to Rabbi Nathan clearly found inadequate the mode of intelligible discourse and the medium of expression selected by the framers of the document they chose to extend. The later writers possessed a message they deemed integral to that unfolding Torah of Moses at Sinai.   They resorted to a mode of intelligible discourse, narrative, that conveyed propositions with great clarity, deeming the medium – again, narrative – a vehicle for conveying propositions from heart to heart. Not only so, but among the narratives utilized in their composition, they selected one for closest attention and narrative development.   The sage story took pride of place in its paramount position in The Fathers According to Rabbi Nathan, and that same subclassification of narrative bore messages conveyed, in the document before us, in no other medium. The framers made ample use of formerly neglected matters of intellect, aesthetics, and theology, specifically, to compose their ideas through a mode of cogent thought, so as to construct intelligible discourse through a medium, meant to speak with immediacy and power to convey a message of critical urgency.

Accordingly, they found place for all four types of narrative, and, of greatest interest, they made use of the sage story to convey powerful propositions lacking all precedent in The Fathers and, in context, therefore of an utterly fresh order. That they made the shift from a document that articulated propositions principally through aphorisms, to one that made points through narrative and particularly through sage stories is entirely clear. Three traits define the sage story in this document.

[1] The story about a sage has a beginning, middle, and end, and the story about a sage also rests not only on verbal exchanges ("he said to him..., he said to him..."), but on (described) action.

[2] The story about a sage unfolds from a point of tension and conflict to a clear resolution and remission of the conflict.

[3] The story about a sage rarely invokes a verse of Scripture and never serves to prove a proposition concerning the meaning of a verse of Scripture.

What about Scripture stories? The traits of stories about scriptural figures and themes prove opposite:

[1] In the story about a scriptural hero there is no beginning, middle, and end, and little action. The burden of the narrative is carried by "he said to him..., he said to him...." Described action is rare and plays slight role in the unfolding of the narrative. Often the narrative consists of little more than a setting for a saying, and the point of the narrative is conveyed not through what is told but through the cited saying.

[2] The story about a scriptural hero is worked out as a tableau, with description of the components of the stationary tableau placed at the center. There is little movement, no point of tension that is resolved.

[3] The story about a scriptural hero always invokes verses from Scripture and makes the imputation of meaning to those verses the center of interest.

So The Fathers According to Rabbi Nathan systematically enriches The Fathers with a variety of narratives, each with its own conventions. When the narrators wished to talk about sages, they invoked one set of narrative conventions, deemed appropriate to that topic, and when they turned to make up stories on scriptural heroes and topics, they appealed to quite different narrative conventions.

Rhetoric

The forms of The Fathers are three: the list of names + attribution + wise sayings; secondary amplifications of sayings; and the list of items of a single classification. The forms of The Fathers According to Rabbi Nathan differ only in one way:

[4] The appendix, with the subdivision, the genre of biographical tale, following diverse formal patterns or no clear pattern at all. This may include a parable, a secondary restatement as a proposition of a lesson that is originally conveyed as a story.

The appendix is not a form, of course, but appendices are highly formalized. Ordinarily they are made up of the familiar form: citation of a verse of Scripture, followed by secondary expansion of the cited verse. That is to say, the form that follows the pattern of citing a statement of The Fathers and then saying, "how so?" or "this teaches that...," finds its counterpart in the entirely familiar formal pattern of citation and gloss of Scripture. Indeed, we may say that The Fathers According to Rabbi Nathan serves The Fathers much as do the two Talmuds serve the Mishnah and the several compilations of scriptural exegeses serve Scripture. So what makes the appendix different in its formal traits is solely the subdivision, *the story* – and that does not constitute a difference in form at all.

Logic of Coherent Discourse

The medium and the message of The Fathers According to Rabbi Nathan appeal to a mode of thought different from the logic that dominates in The Fathers. What holds together those many units of discourse that constitute more than sequences of unrelated declarative sentences is the teleological logic of narrative. Narrative may encompass one of four modes of the concrete portrayal of a message, noted in the beginning of this chapter: [1] the parable; [2] the precipitant: the narrative setting for, or formal precipitant of, a saying; [3] the (ordinarily legal, but sometimes moral) precedent; [4] and the story. The story furthermore is divided into two subspecies: [4A] scriptural or Scripture story, [4B] sagacious or sage story.

THE PARABLE: A parable unfolds through resort to narrative. There was a king who had such and so, who said such and such, who did so and so – with the result that such and such happened. The parable is a narrative in that the appeal for cogency is to teleology, and the proposition of the parable emerges (whether made explicit or not) as a self-evident exemplification of the teleology at hand. So the explanation, the principle of cogency, derives from the order of events: do this with that result, say this with that consequence.

THE PRECIPITANT: THE NARRATIVE SETTING FOR A SAYING: What I call formal setting, or "precipitant," for a saying merely portrays a situation to which a setting pertains, for example, "He saw a skull and said...." That hardly adds up to a substantial narrative, let alone a sustained story, since nothing happens to draw out the significance of the event, "he saw," but it does demand classification as a narrative, because something has happened, not merely been said. Such a formal setting for a saying may prove substantial, but it will not constitute a narrative in the way that a parable or a sage or other kind of story does, because not the action but the saying forms the focus of interest, and the potentialities of tension and resolution constituted by the precipitating action ("one day he saw a skull and said...") are never explored.

A PRECEDENT OR ILLUSTRATION OF A LAW: A precedent narrates a case, often enough in the form of a tale of something done, not merely said. The setting is always discourse on the law, but what marks the narrative as precedent as different from the narrative as story is not its setting but the definitive narrative convention that pertains in the precedent but not in the story (sage, scriptural, or other). Specifically, the precedent will portray a tableau of *completed action*, in which the tension is established not by the action but by the (sage's) ruling, and in which the resolution of the tension is accomplished solely by the same component, the decision of the sage. In line with this convention that nothing really happen, in the precedent we rarely find a beginning, middle, and end, such as we always find in a parable and a story. The precedent or illustration is concrete and specific, in the way a story is, but not to a distinctive named person and time and place, in the way a story is. The precedent, unlike a story, is paradigmatic and makes a general point, rather than historical and particular to a distinctive situation. A precedent or illustration of the law is like a parable in that it presents no concrete details that allow us to identify a particular place or actor.

THE STORY (SCRIPTURAL OR SAGE): Among narratives, we may always distinguish a story from any other type of narrative in one fundamental and definitive way. Its importance requires emphasis: while meaning to provide a good example of how one should behave, the teller of a story always deals with a concrete person and a particular incident. The person is concrete in that he (in our document there is not a single story about a woman) is always specified by name. It concerns a particular incident in that the viewpoint of the narrator makes clear the one-timeness and specificity of the event that is reported. The story always happens in historical time, and the point it wishes to make is subordinate to the description of action, the development of a point of tension, at which the story commences, and its resolution, at which the story concludes: beginning, middle, and end.

Topical Program

The topical program of The Fathers According to Rabbi Nathan in particular emerges only in identifying topics treated in the successor compilations but not in the principal one. Points of emphasis in The Fathers lacking all counterpart in restatement and development in the Fathers According to Rabbi Nathan make three points. First, the study of the Torah alone does not suffice. One has also to make an honest living through work. In what is particular to The Fathers According to Rabbi Nathan we find not that point but its opposite: one should study the Torah and other things will take care of themselves – a claim of a more supernatural character than the one in The Fathers. A second point of clear interest in the earlier document to which, in the later one, we find no response tells sages to accommodate their wishes to those of the community at large, to accept the importance of the government, to work in community, to practice self-abnegation and restraint in favor of the wishes of others. The sage here is less a supernatural figure than a political leader, eager to conciliate and reconcile the other. The third and most important, indicative shift in the later document imparts to the teleological question an eschatological answer altogether lacking in the earlier one.

If we were to ask the authorship of Avot to spell out their teleology, they would draw our attention to the numerous sayings about this life's being a time of preparation for the life of the world to come, on the one side, and to judgment and eternal life, on the other. The focus is on the individual and how he or she lives in this world and prepares for the next. The category is the individual, and, commonly in the two documents before us when we speak of the individual, we also tend to find the language of "this world" and "the world to come," *olam hazzeh*, *olam habbah.* The sequence of sayings about this world and the next form a stunning contrast to the ones about this age and the next age, *olam hazzeh, le'atid labo.* In general, though not invariably, the shift in language draws in its wake a shift in social category, from individual to social entity of group, nation, or people. The word "olam" bears two meanings, "world," and "age." In context, when we find the word bearing the sense of "world," the category under discussion is the private person, and where the required sense, in English, is "age," then – as a rough rule of thumb – what is promised is for the nation.

We can tell that the definitive category is social, therefore national, when at stake is the fate not of the private person but of holy Israel. The concern then is what will happen to the nation in time to come, meaning the coming age, not the coming life of the resurrection. The systemic teleology shifts its focus to the holy people, and, alongside, to the national history of the holy people – now and in the age to come. So in the movement from this world and the world to come, to this age and the age to come, often expressed as the coming future, *le'atid labo,* we note an accompanying categorical shift in the definitive context: from individual and private life of home and family, to society and historical, public life. That shift then characterizes the teleological movement, as much as the categorical change. And, as we see, it is contained both in general and in detail in the differences we have noticed between The Fathers and The Fathers According to Rabbi Nathan.

The national-eschatological interest of the later document, with its focus on living only in the Land of Israel, on the one side, and its contrast between this age, possessed by the gentiles, and the age to come, in which redeemed Israel will enjoy a paramount position, which has no counterpart in the earlier composition, emerges not only in sayings but also in stories about the critical issue, the destruction of Jerusalem and the loss of the Temple, along with the concomitant matter, associated with the former stories, about repentance and how it is achieved at this time.

Yet a further point of development lies in the notion that study of the Torah combined with various virtues, for example, good deeds, fear of sin, suffices, with a concomitant assurance that making a living no longer matters. Here, too, the new medium of the later document – the stories about sages – bears the new message. For that conviction emerges not only explicitly – for example, in the sayings of Hananiah about the power of Torah study to take away many sources of suffering, Judah b. Ilai's that one should treat words of the Torah as the principal, earning a living as trivial, and so on – but also in the detail that both Aqiba and Eliezer began poor but through their mastery of Torah ended rich.

The Fathers According to Rabbi Nathan differs from The Fathers in one aspect so fundamental as to change the face of the base document completely. While the earlier authorship took slight interest in lives and deeds of sages, the later one contributed in a systematic and orderly manner the color and life of biography to the named but faceless sages of The Fathers. The stories about sages make points that correspond to positions taken in statements of viewpoints particular to The Fathers According to Rabbi Nathan. The Fathers presents an ideal of the sage as model for the everyday life of the individual, who must study the Torah and also work, and through the good life prepare now for life after death, while The Fathers According to Rabbi Nathan has a different conception of the sage, of the value and meaning of the study of the Torah, and of the center of interest – and also has selected a new medium for the expression of its distinctive conception. To spell this out:

[1]   The sage is now – in the Fathers According to Rabbi Nathan – not a judge and teacher alone but also a supernatural figure.

[2]   Study of the Torah in preference to making a living promises freedom from the conditions of natural life.

[3]   Israel as the holy people seen as a supernatural social entity takes center stage.

And these innovative points are conveyed not only in sayings but in stories about sages.

What follows is that the medium not only carries a new message but also forms a component of that new message. The sage as a supernatural figure now presents Torah teachings through what he does, not only through what he says. Therefore telling stories about what sages did and the circumstances in which they made their sayings forms part of the Torah, in a way in which, in the earlier document, it clearly did not. The interest in stories about sages proves therefore not merely literary or formal; it is more than a new way of conveying an old message. Stories about the sages are told because sages stand for a message that can emerge only in stories and not in sayings alone. So we turn to a close reading of the stories themselves to review that message and find out why through stories in particular the message now emerges. For what we see is nothing short of a new mode of revelation, that is, of conveying and imparting God's will in the Torah.

People told stories because they wanted to think about history, and, in their setting, history emerged in an account of what happened, with an implicit message of the meaning of events conveyed in the story as well.

They further conceived of the social entity, Israel, as an extended family, children of a single progenitor, Abraham, with his sons, Isaac and Jacob. Consequently, when they told stories, they centered on family history. That accounts in general for the details of what the authorship of The Fathers According to Rabbi Nathan have chosen to add to the topical program of The Fathers. The sage in the system of The Fathers According to Rabbi Nathan constituted the supernatural father, who replaced the natural one; events in the life of the sage constituted happenings in the history of the family-nation, Israel. So history blended with family, and family with Torah study. The national, salvific history of the nation-family, Israel, took place in such events as the origins of the sage, meaning, his beginnings in Torah study; the sagacity of the sage, the counterpart to what we should call social history; the doings of the sage in great turnings in the family's history, including, especially, the destruction of the Temple, now perceived as final and decisive; and the death of the sage, while engaged in Torah study. And these form the four classifications of story in this document.

II. Unarticulated Premises: The Givens of Religious Conduct

Making a fence around the Torah does not yield further exemplification of special interest.

III. Unarticulated Premises: The Givens of Religious Conviction

1. The nature of Adam from the very beginning was to sin, and Adam could not abide in Eden for even a day:

I

XII.1 A. What was the order of the creation of the first Man? [The entire sequence of events of the creation and fall of Man and Woman took place on a single day, illustrating a series of verses of Psalms that are liturgically utilized on the several days of the week.]

B. In the first hour [of the sixth day, on which Man was made] the dirt for making him was gathered, in the second, his form was shaped, in the third, he was turned into a mass of dough, in the fourth, his limbs were made, in the fifth, his various apertures were opened up, in the sixth, breath was put into him, in the seventh, he stood on his feet, in the eighth, Eve was made as his match, in the ninth, he was put into the Garden of Eden, in the tenth, he was given the commandment, in the eleventh, he turned rotten, in the twelfth, he was driven out and went his way.

C. This carries out the verse: "But Man does not lodge overnight in honor" (Ps. 49:13).

D. On the first day of the week [with reference to the acts of creation done on that day], what Psalm is to be recited? "The earth is the Lord's and the fullness thereof, the world and they who dwell in it"

(Ps. 24:1). For [God] is the one who owns it and transfers ownership of it, and he is the one who will judge the world.

E.   On the second day? "Great is the Lord and greatly to be praised in the city of our God" (Ps. 48:2). He divided everything he had made [between sea and dry land] and was made king over his world.

F.   On the third day? "God is standing in the congregation of the mighty, in the midst of the mighty he will judge" (Ps. 82:1). He created the sea and the dry land and folded up the land to its place, leaving a place for his congregation.

G.   On the fourth day? "God of vengeance, O Lord, God of vengeance," appear (Ps. 94:1). He created the sun, moon, stars, and planets, which give light to the world but He is going to exact vengeance from those who serve them.]

H.   On the fifth? "Sing aloud to God our strength, shout to the God of Jacob" (Ps. 81:2). He created the fowl, fish, mammals of the sea, who sing aloud in the world [praises of God].

I.   On the sixth? "The Lord reigns, clothed in majesty, the Lord is clothed, girded in strength, yes, the world is established and cannot be moved" (Ps. 93:1). On that day he completed all his work and arose and took his seat on the heights of the world.

J.   On the seventh? "A Psalm, a song for the Sabbath day" (Ps. 92:1). It is a day that is wholly a Sabbath, on which there is no eating drinking, or conducting of business, but the righteous are seated in retinue with their crowns on their heads and derive sustenance from the splendor of God's presence, as it is said, "And they beheld God and ate and drank" (Ex. 24:11), like the ministering angels.

K.   And [reverting back to B] why [was man created last]?

L.   So that [immediately upon creation on the sixth day] he might forthwith take up his Sabbath meal.

I

XIV.1 A.   On the very same day Man was formed, on the very same day Man was made, on the very same day his form was shaped, on the very same day he was turned into a mass of dough, on the very same day his limbs were made and his various apertures were opened up, on the very same day breath was put into him, on the very same day he stood on his feet, on the very same day Eve was matched for him, on the very same day he was put into the Garden of Eden, on the very same day he was given the commandment, on the very same day he went bad, on the very same day he was driven out and went his way,

B.   thereby illustrating the verse, "Man does not lodge overnight in honor" (Ps. 49:24).

IV. Matters of Philosophy, Natural Science and Metaphysics

Nothing pertains here.

32

The Fathers According to Rabbi Nathan Chapter Two

I. Unarticulated Premises: The Givens of Religious Conduct

Making a fence around the Torah requires extending the law to areas that, by strict rule, are permitted; by doing so, one makes certain of not violating those rules' main point:

II

I.1   A.   What sort of fence did the Torah make around its words?

        B.   Lo, Scripture says, "To a woman during the unclean time of her menstrual period you shall not draw near" (Lev. 18:17).

        C.   Is it possible to suppose that one may nonetheless hug and kiss her and exchange billydoos with her?

        D.   Scripture says, "you shall not draw near."

        E.   Is it nonetheless possible to suppose that if she is fully clothed, one may sleep with her in the same bed?

        F.   Scripture says, "you shall not draw near."

        G.   Is it possible to suppose that a woman my pretty her face and put on eye makeup?

        H.   Scripture says, "And of her that is sick with her impurity" (Lev. 15:33), meaning, all the days of her menstrual period she shall be put away.

        I.   On this basis they have said: whoever neglects herself during her menstrual period enjoys the approbation of sages, and whoever pretties herself during her menstrual period does not enjoy the approbation of sages.

I.2   A.   There is the precedent of a man who studied much Scripture, repeated much Mishnah, extensively served as a disciple of sages, but died when his years were only half done, and his wife took his tefillin and made the circuit of synagogues and schoolhouses, crying and weeping, saying to them, "My lords, it is written in the Torah, 'For it is your life and the length of your days' (Deut. 30:20).

B.   "On what account did my husband, who studied much Scripture, repeated much Mishnah, extensively served as a disciple of sages, die when his years were only half done?"

C.   No one knew what to answer her. But one time Elijah, of blessed memory, was appointed to deal with her, saying to her, "My daughter, on what account are you crying and weeping?"

D.   She said to him, "My lord, my husband studied much Scripture, repeated much Mishnah, extensively served as a disciple of sages, but died when his years were only half done."

E.   He said to her, "When you were in your period, on the first three days of your period, what was your practice?"

F.   She said to him, "My lord, God forbid, he never touched me, even with his little finger. But this is what he said to me, 'Do not touch a thing, perhaps you may come into doubt about something.'"

G.   "As to the last days of your period, what was your practice?"

H.   She said to him, "My lord, I ate with him, drank with him, and in my clothing slept with him in the same bed, and, while his flesh touched mine, he never had the intention of any inappropriate action [such as sexual relations before the period had fully ended]."

I.   He said to her, "Blessed be the Omnipresent, who killed him. For so is it written in the Torah: 'To a woman during the unclean time of her menstrual period you shall not draw near' (Lev. 18:17)."

II. Unarticulated Premises: The Givens of Religious Conviction

I find nothing of theological interest here.

III. Matters of Philosophy, Natural Science and Metaphysics

There is no reason to expect materials of philosophical interest.

33

The Fathers According to Rabbi Nathan Chapter Three

I find no broad and general principles requiring analysis.

34

The Fathers According to
Rabbi Nathan Chapter Four

I. Unarticulated Premises: The Givens of Religious Conduct

I find nothing of halakhic interest.

II. Unarticulated Premises: The Givens of Religious Conviction

1. The welfare of nature and humanity depends upon the maintenance of the Temple offerings:

IV

IV.1   A.   ...**on the Temple service**: how so?

B.   So long as the Temple service of the house of the sanctuary went on, the world was blessed for its inhabitants and rain came down in the proper time.

C.   For it is said, "To love the Lord your God and to serve him with all your heart and with all your soul that I will provide the rain of your land in its season, the former rain and the latter rain...and I will provide grass in your fields for your cattle" (Deut. 11:13-14).

D.   But when the Temple service of the house of the sanctuary ceased to go on, the world was not blessed for its inhabitants, and rain did not come down in the proper time,

E.   as it is said, "Take heed to yourselves lest your heart be deceived...and he shut up the heaven so that there shall be no rain" (Deut. 11:16-17).

III. Matters of Philosophy, Natural Science and Metaphysics

We may hardly anticipate materials for this rubric.

35

The Fathers According to Rabbi Nathan Chapter Five

This chapter presents nothing relevant to our inquiry.

36

The Fathers According to Rabbi Nathan Chapter Six

The chapter presents nothing relevant to this study.

37

The Fathers According to Rabbi Nathan Chapter Seven

I find nothing of interest in this chapter.

38

The Fathers According to Rabbi Nathan Chapter Eight

I. Unarticulated Premises: The Givens of Religious Conduct

There is nothing here of halakhic consequence.

II. Unarticulated Premises: The Givens of Religious Conviction

1. God is present where and when and among those by whom the Torah is studied, and a reward is given for the learning:

VIII

III.1 A. In the case of three disciples in session and occupied with study of the Torah, the Holy One, blessed be He, credits it to them as if they formed a single band before him,

B. as it is said, "He who builds his upper chambers in the heaven and has founded his band upon the earth, he who calls for the waters of the sea and pours them out upon the face of the earth, the Lord is his name" (Amos 9:6).

C. Thus you have learned that in the case of three disciples in session and occupied with study of the Torah, the Holy One, blessed be He, credits it to them as if they formed a single band before him.

III.2 A. In the case of two disciples in session and occupied with study of the Torah, their reward is received on high,

B. as it is said, "Then they who feared the Lord spoke one with another, and the Lord heard...and a book of remembrance was written before him for those who feared the Lord and who gave thought to his name" (Mal. 3:16).

C. Who are those referred to as "they who feared the Lord"?'

D. They are the ones who reach a decision, saying, "Let us go and free those who are imprisoned and redeem those who have been kidnapped for ransom," and the Holy One, blessed be He, gave sufficient power in their hands to do so, and they go and do it right away.

	E.	And who are those referred to as "they who gave thought to his name"?
	F.	They are the ones who reckon in their hearts, saying, "Let us go and free those who are imprisoned and redeem those who have been kidnapped for ransom," and the Holy One, blessed be He, did not give sufficient power in their hands to do so, so an angel came and beat them down to the ground.
III.3	A.	In the case of an individual disciple in session and occupied with study of the Torah, his reward is received on high,
	B.	as it is said, "Though he sit alone and keep silence, surely he has laid up [a reward] for him" (Lam. 3:28).
	C.	The matter may be conveyed in a parable: to what is it comparable?
	D.	To someone who had a young child, whom he left at home when he went out to the market. The son went and took a scroll and set it between his knees and sat and meditated on it.
	E.	When his father came back from the marketplace, he said, "See my little son, whom I left when I went out to the marketplace. What has he done on his own! He has studied and taken the scroll and set it between his knees, going into session and meditating on it."
	F.	So you have learned that even an individual disciple who has gone into session and occupied with study of the Torah, receives his reward received on high.

III. Matters of Philosophy, Natural Science and Metaphysics

The discussion of the right attitude and action does not rise to a philosophical level.

39

The Fathers According to Rabbi Nathan Chapter Nine

The chapter contains nothing relevant to our study.

40

The Fathers According to Rabbi Nathan Chapter Ten

The chapter contains nothing relevant to our study.

41

The Fathers According to
Rabbi Nathan Chapter Eleven

The chapter contains nothing relevant to our study.

42

The Fathers According to Rabbi Nathan Chapter Twelve

The chapter presents nothing both relevant and fresh.

43

The Fathers According to
Rabbi Nathan Chapter Thirteen

This brief chapter contains nothing relevant to this inquiry.

44

The Fathers According to
Rabbi Nathan Chapter Fourteen

Premises of a legal, theological, or philosophical order are difficult to identify here.

45

The Fathers According to
Rabbi Nathan Chapter Fifteen

There is nothing here that yields a premise of consequence.

46

The Fathers According to
Rabbi Nathan Chapter Sixteen

I. Unarticulated Premises: The Givens of Religious Conduct

Premises concerning laws do not emerge here.

II. Unarticulated Premises: The Givens of Religious Conviction

1. It is natural for human beings to sin; the propensity to do evil is built into their beings; it is not natural for them to carry out religious deeds or do good:

XVI

III.1   A.   **Desire of bad things:** how so?

        B.   The impulse to do evil is thirteen years older than the impulse to do good.

        C.   From the mother's womb it grows and develops with a person.

        D   If one began to profane the Sabbath, it does not stop him. If he wanted to kill, it does not stop him. If he goes to commit a transgression [of a sexual character], it does not stop him.

        E.   After thirteen years the impulse to do good is born. When the man then violates the Sabbath, it says to him, "Empty head, lo, Scripture says, 'Those who profane it will surely die' (Ex. 31:11)."

        F.   When the man then kills, it says to him, "Empty head, lo, Scripture says, 'One who sheds man's blood by man his blood will be shed' (Gen. 9:6)."

        G.   When he goes to commit a transgression, it says to him, "Empty head, lo, Scripture says, 'The adulterer and the adulteress will surely die' (Lev. 20:10)."

III.2   A.   When a man arouses himself and goes to commit fornication, all of his limbs obey him, because the impulse to do evil is king over the two hundred and forty-eight limbs.

        B.   But when he goes to carry out a religious duty, all his limbs [Goldin:] begin to drag, because the impulse to do evil from the womb is king over the two hundred and forty-eight limbs that are in a man.

C.   The impulse to do good is only like one who is imprisoned, as it is said, "For out of prison he came forth to be king" (Qoh. 4:14), referring to the impulse to do good.

2.   But great masters of the Torah do overcome their desire to sin:

XVI

IV.4   A.   And do not take as surprising the case of R. Aqiba, for lo, there is R. Eliezer the Elder, who is still greater than he, who raised the daughter of his sister for thirteen years with him in the same bed, until the puberty signs appeared.

B.   He said to her, "Go, marry a man."

C.   She said to him, "Am I not your slave girl, a handmaiden there to wash the feet of your disciple[s]?"

D.   He said to her, "My daughter, I am an old man. Go and marry a youngster like yourself."

E.   She said to him, "Have I not said to you, Am I not your slave girl, a handmaiden there to wash the feet of your disciple[s]?"

F.   When he had heard what she said, he asked permission of her, betrothed her, and had sexual relations with her [as his bride].

III. Matters of Philosophy, Natural Science and Metaphysics

The chapter contains nothing philosophical.

47

The Fathers According to
Rabbi Nathan Chapter Seventeen

I. Unarticulated Premises: The Givens of Religious Conduct

Nothing qualifies.

II. Unarticulated Premises: The Givens of Religious Conviction

1. Incidents in everyday life clarify the meaning of the Torah:

XVII

III.1 A. One time Rabban Yohanan ben Zakkai was walking in the marketplace. He saw a young girl gathering barley from under the hooves of the cattle of Arabs. He said to her, "My daughter, who are you?"

B. She kept silent.

C. Again he said to her, "My daughter, who are you?"

D. She kept silent.

E. She said to him, "Hold it a minute." Then she covered herself with her hair and sat down before him. She said to him, "My lord, I am the daughter of Nakdimon b. Gurion."

F. He said to her, "My daughter, what ever became of the wealth of your father's house?"

G. She said to him, "My lord, is it not an apophthegm in Jerusalem: [Goldin:] 'Money will keep if you don't keep it,' and some say, '...if you give charity.'"

H. He said to her, "What ever happened to your father-in-law's money?"

I. She said to him, "My lord, this came and took the other along with it."

J. At that moment said Rabban Yohanan ben Zakkai to his disciples, "For my entire life I have been reciting this verse of Scripture, 'If you do not know, O you fairest among women, go your way forth by the footsteps of the flock and feed your kids beside the shepherds' tents' (Song 1:8).

K. "But I never learned what it meant until I came to this day and I have now learned what it means.

L. "For the Israelites have fallen subject to the most despicable of all nations, and not only to that despicable nation alone, but even to the dung of their cattle."

M. The girl further said to him, "My lord, do you remember when you inscribed your seal on my marriage contract?"

N. He said to her, "Yes I do," and he said to the disciples, "By the Temple service! I inscribed my seal on this girl's marriage contract, and in it was written the sum of a thousand thousand golden denars in Tyrian coinage.

O. "In the time of this girl's father's household they never went from their houses to the house of the sanctuary before woolen rugs were spread out [for them to walk on]."

III. Matters of Philosophy, Natural Science and Metaphysics

Nothing is relevant.

48

The Fathers According to
Rabbi Nathan Chapter Eighteen

The chapter contributes nothing to our study.

49

The Fathers According to
Rabbi Nathan Chapter Nineteen

The chapter contributes nothing to our study.

50

The Fathers According to Rabbi Nathan Chapter Twenty

I. Unarticulated Premises: The Givens of Religious Conduct

The chapter presents nothing of interest.

II. Unarticulated Premises: The Givens of Religious Conviction

1. The Torah purifies the heart and removes the impulse to do evil:

XX

I.1   A.   R. Hananiah, prefect of the priests, says, "Whoever places the teachings of the Torah upon his heart is relieved of many [Goldin:] preoccupations:

      B.   "Those of hunger, silliness, libido, impulse to do evil, a bad woman, idle nonsense, the yoke of mortals.

      C.   "For so it is written in the book of Psalms by King David of Israel: 'The precepts of the Lord are right, rejoicing the heart, the commandment of the Lord is pure, enlightening the eyes' (Ps. 19:9).

      D.   "And whoever does not place the teachings of the Torah upon his heart is burdened by many [Goldin:] preoccupations:

      E.   "those of perpetual hunger, silliness, libido, the evil impulse, a bad woman, idle nonsense, the yoke of mortals.

      F.   "For so it is written in the Repetition of the Torah [the book of Deuteronomy] by Moses, our lord, 'And they shall be upon you for a sign and for a wonder, and upon your descendants forever, because you did not serve the Lord your God with joyfulness, and with gladness of heart, by reason of the abundance of all things, therefore you shall serve your enemy whom the Lord shall send against you, in hunger and in thirst and in nakedness and in want of all things' (Deut. 28:46-48)."

III. Matters of Philosophy, Natural Science and Metaphysics

The chapter contains nothing relevant.

51

The Fathers According to
Rabbi Nathan Chapter Twenty-One

This chapter makes no contribution to our study.

52

The Fathers According to
Rabbi Nathan Chapter Twenty-Two

This chapter makes no contribution to our study.

53

The Fathers According to
Rabbi Nathan Chapter Twenty-Three

This chapter makes no contribution to our study.

54

The Fathers According to
Rabbi Nathan Chapter Twenty-Four

This chapter makes no contribution to our study.

55

The Fathers According to
Rabbi Nathan Chapter Twenty-Five

Nothing in this chapter serves our inquiry.

56

The Fathers According to
Rabbi Nathan Chapter Twenty-Six

This chapter contributes nothing to our inquiry.

57

The Fathers According to
Rabbi Nathan Chapter Twenty-Seven

This chapter contributes nothing to our inquiry.

58

The Fathers According to Rabbi Nathan Chapter Twenty-Eight

I. Unarticulated Premises: The Givens of Religious Conduct

I find nothing of halakhic concern in this chapter.

II. Unarticulated Premises: The Givens of Religious Conviction

1. What makes Israel special is the love for, and wisdom deriving from, the Torah. Various nations' traits characterize their history as well:

XXVIII

I.1   A.   R. Nathan says, "You have no love like the love for the Torah, wisdom like the wisdom of the Land of Israel, beauty like the beauty of Jerusalem, wealth like the wealth of Rome, power like the power of Persia, lewdness like the lewdness of the Arabs, arrogance like the arrogance of Elam, hypocrisy like the hypocrisy of Babylonia –

      B.   ("as it is said, 'And he said to me, to build her a house in the land of Shinar' ([Zech. 5:11]) –

      C.   "or witchcraft like the witchcraft of Egypt."

III. Matters of Philosophy, Natural Science and Metaphysics

We cannot expect to identify pertinent compositions here.

59

The Fathers According to
Rabbi Nathan Chapter Twenty-Nine

The chapter contributes nothing to our study.

60

The Fathers According to
Rabbi Nathan Chapter Thirty

The chapter contributes nothing to our study.

61

The Fathers According to Rabbi Nathan Chapter Thirty-One

I. Unarticulated Premises: The Givens of Religious Conduct

I find nothing of legal consequence here.

II. Unarticulated Premises: The Givens of Religious Conviction

1. Human life is holy. Every individual is sacred and of infinite worth; every action is consequential; every sin is consequential; the stakes are always high, and God is always involved in what people do:

XXXI

I.1 A. By ten acts of speech was the world made:

     B. Now why do people need to be told that? It is to teach you that whoever carries out a single religious duty, whoever observes a single Sabbath, whoever saves a single life [Goldin, p. 204, n. 4 does not read "of Israel"] is credited by Scripture as though he had sustained the entire world that was created by ten words.

     C. And whoever commits a single transgression, whoever violates a single Sabbath, whoever destroys a single life, is credited by Scripture as though he had destroyed the entire world that was created by ten words.

I.2 A. So we find in the case of Cain, who killed Abel his brother, as it is said, "The voice of the bloods of your brother cry out to me" (Gen. 4:10).

     B. He spilled the blood of a single human being, but Scripture speaks of bloods in the plural.

     C. This teaches that the blood of his children, grandchildren, and all the coming heirs to the end of all generations that were destined to come forth from him, all of them were standing and crying out before the Holy One, blessed be He.

     D. So you learn that one person is equivalent to all the works of creation.

I.3   A.   R. Nehemiah says, "How do we know that a single person is equivalent to all the words of creation?

       B.   "As it is said, 'This is the book of the generations of man, in the day that God created man, in the likeness of God he made him' (Gen. 5:1), and, elsewhere, 'These are the generations of heaven and earth when they were created' (Gen. 12:4).

       C.   "Just as in that latter passage we speak of creating and making, so in the former were creating and making.

       D.   "This teaches that the Holy One, blessed be He, showed him all the generations that were destined to come forth from him, as though they were standing and [Goldin:] rejoicing before him."

       E.   Some say that he showed him only the righteous alone, as it is written, "All those who were written unto life in Jerusalem" (Isa. 4:3).

III. Matters of Philosophy, Natural Science and Metaphysics

While the statements concerning the worth of the human being bear philosophical consequence, they are set forth in a theological context and do not generate speculation, for example, concerning man as the measure of all things or other moral principles.

62

The Fathers According to
Rabbi Nathan Chapter Thirty-Two

The chapter yields no unfamiliar premises or presuppositions.

63

The Fathers According to
Rabbi Nathan Chapter Thirty-Three

I. Unarticulated Premises: The Givens of Religious Conduct

There is nothing of halakhic interest here.

II. Unarticulated Premises: The Givens of Religious Conviction

1. The merit of the fathers sustains the children for generations to come; what Abraham did provoked an exact correspondence in God's dealing with the Israelites in Egypt; Israel's history spins out the effects of the ancestors' merits:

XXXIII

II.1 A. Ten trials were inflicted upon Abraham, our father, before the Holy One, blessed be He, and in all of them he came out whole.

B. These are they: two in the passage, "Go forth" [Goldin: twice, when ordered to move on]; two in connection with his two sons; two in connection with his two wives; one with the kings; one in the covenant between the pieces; one in the furnace of the Chaldeans; one in connection with circumcision.

C. And why all of these trials?

D. So that when Abraham our father would come to receive his reward, when the nations of the world would complain, "More than all of us, more than everyone, Abraham is worthy of receiving his reward."

E. And in connection with him, Scripture says, "Go your way, eat your bread with joy and drink your wine with a merry heart, for God has already accepted your works" (Qoh. 9:7).

III.1 A. In response to the ten trials inflicted upon Abraham, our father, from all of which he emerged whole, the Holy One, blessed be He, performed ten miracles for his children in Egypt.

B. And corresponding to them also, the Holy One, blessed be He, brought ten plagues on the Egyptians in Egypt.

C.   And corresponding to them also, ten miracles were done for the Israelites at the sea.

D.   And corresponding to them also, he brought ten plagues on the Egyptians at the sea.

III. Matters of Philosophy, Natural Science and Metaphysics

Obviously, we can expect to find nothing of philosophical concern.

64

The Fathers According to
Rabbi Nathan Chapter Thirty-Four

I. Unarticulated Premises: The Givens of Religious Conduct

I find no incidents of consequence here.

II. Unarticulated Premises: The Givens of Religious Conviction

1. God entered the world on account of Israel, and God departed from the world because of Israel's actions; the center of God's presence was the Temple in its time; but the presence abandoned the Temple in due course:

XXXIV

VIII.1 A. There were ten descents that the Presence of God made into the world.

B. One into the Garden of Eden, as it says, "And they heard the sound of God walking in the garden" (Gen. 3:5).

C. One in the generation of the tower of Babylon, as it is said, "And the Lord came down to see the city and the tower" (Gen. 11:5).

D. One in Sodom: "I shall now go down and see whether it is in accord with the cry that has come to me" (Gen. 18:21).

E. One in Egypt: "I shall go down and save them from the hand of the Egyptians" (Ex. 3:8).

F. One at the sea: "He bowed the heavens also and came down" (2 Sam. 22:10).

G. One at Sinai: "And the Lord came down onto Mount Sinai" (Ex. 19:20).

H. One in the pillar of cloud: "And the Lord came down in a pillar" (Num. 11:25).

I. One in the Temple: "This gate will be closed and will not be open for the Lord, God of Israel, has come in through it" (Ezek. 44:2).

J.   And one is destined to take place in the time of Gog and Magog: "And his feet shall stand that day on the mount of Olives" (Zech. 14:4).

IX.1   A.   In ten upward stages the Presence of God departed, from one place to the next: from the ark cover to the cherub, from the cherub to the threshold of the Temple building; from the threshold of the Temple to the two cherubim; from the two cherubim to the roof of the sanctuary; from the roof of the sanctuary to the wall of the Temple court; from the wall of the Temple court to the altar; from the altar to the city; from the city to the Temple mount; from the Temple mount to the wilderness.

B.   From the ark cover to the cherub: "And he rode upon a cherub and flew" (2 Sam. 22:11).

C.   From the cherub to the threshold of the Temple building: "And the glory of the Lord mounted up from the cherub to the threshold of the house" (Ezek. 10:45).

D.   From the threshold of the temple to the two cherubim: "And the glory of the Lord went forth from off the threshold of the house and stood over the cherubim" (Ezek. 10:18).

E.   From the two cherubim to the roof of the sanctuary: "It is better to dwell in a corner of the housetop" (Prov. 21:9).

F.   From the roof of the sanctuary to the wall of the Temple court: "And behold the Lord stood beside a wall made by a plumbline" (Amos 7:7).

G.   From the wall of the Temple court to the altar: "I saw the Lord standing beside the altar" (Amos 9:1).

H.   From the altar to the city: "Hark, the Lord cries to the city" (Mic. 6:9).

I.   From the city to the Temple mount: "And the glory of the Lord went up from the midst of the city and stood upon the mountain" (Ezek. 11:23).

J.   From the temple mount to the wilderness: "It is better to dwell in a desert land" (Prov. 21:19).

K.   And then to on high: "I will go and return to my place" (Hos. 5:15).

III. Matters of Philosophy, Natural Science and Metaphysics

There is nothing of metaphysical interest here.

65

The Fathers According to
Rabbi Nathan Chapter Thirty-Five

The chapter contributes nothing to our study.

66

The Fathers According to Rabbi Nathan Chapter Thirty-Six

The chapter contributes nothing to our survey.

67

The Fathers According to Rabbi Nathan Chapter Thirty-Seven

I. Unarticulated Premises: The Givens of Religious Conduct

The rules of conduct treated here concern ordinary matters and bear no premises of interest.

II. Unarticulated Premises: The Givens of Religious Conviction

1. Humanity is a mixture of heaven and earth, beasts and angels:

XXXVII

II.1 A.   Six traits have been stated with respect to humanity, three like traits of a beast, three like traits of ministering angels.

B.   Three in which humanity is like the beast: people eat and drink like a beast, procreate like a beast, and shit like a beast.

C.   Three in which humanity is like ministering angels: people have understanding like ministering angels, they walk standing up, like ministering angels, and they make use of the Holy Language, like ministering angels.

III. Matters of Philosophy, Natural Science and Metaphysics

It is hopeless to ask this document for statements bearing philosophical premises.

68

The Fathers According to
Rabbi Nathan Chapter Thirty-Eight

I. Unarticulated Premises: The Givens of Religious Conduct

This category does not serve.

II. Unarticulated Premises: The Givens of Religious Conviction

1. Whatever happens in the world is just, and justice is exact and precise:

XXXVIII

VI.1   A.   Exile comes into the world because of those who worship idols, because of fornication, and because of bloodshed, and because of the neglect of the release of the Land [in the year of release].

B.   On account of idolatry, as it is said: "And I will destroy your high places...and I will scatter you among the nations" (Lev. 26:30,33).

C.   Said the Holy One, blessed be He, to Israel, "Since you lust after idolatry, so I shall send you into exile to a place in which there is idolatry.

D.   Therefore it is said, "And I will destroy your high places...and I will scatter you among the nations."

E.   [Following Goldin's ordering of the text:] Because of fornication: Said R. Ishmael b. R. Yosé, "So long as the Israelites are lawless in fornication, the Presence of God takes its leave of them,"

F.   as it is said, "That he not see an unseemly thing in you and turn away from you" (Deut. 23:15).

G.   [Following Goldin:] Because of bloodshed: "So you shall not pollute the land in which you are located, for blood pollutes the land" (Num. 35:33).

H.   Because of neglect of the release of the Land in the year of release: how do we know that that is the case?

I.   "Then shall the land be paid her Sabbaths" (Lev. 26:34).

J.   Said the Holy One, blessed be He, to Israel, "Since you do not propose to give the land its rest, it will give you a rest. For the number of months that you did not give the land rest, it will take a rest on its own.

K.   That is why it is said, "Even then shall the land rest and repay her Sabbaths. As long as it lies desolate it shall have rest, even the rest that it did not have on your sabbaths, when you lived on it" (Lev. 26:35).

III. Matters of Philosophy, Natural Science and Metaphysics

Despite the foregoing statement of mine, I find here nothing of philosophical interest.

69

The Fathers According to
Rabbi Nathan Chapter Thirty-Nine

I. Unarticulated Premises: The Givens of Religious Conduct

No halakhic discussions take place here.

II. Unarticulated Premises: The Givens of Religious Conviction

1. Even though it appears that the wicked prosper and the righteous suffer, this is only for a brief interval; the world to come allows for the balancing of matters, so that the wicked get their just punishment, and the righteous, their just reward:

XXXIX

V.1 A. The repentance of genuinely wicked people suspends [their punishment], but the decree against them has been sealed.

B. The prosperity of the wicked in the end will go sour.

C. Dominion buries those that hold it.

D. Repentance suspends [punishment] and the Day of Atonement achieves atonement.

E. Repentance suspends [punishment] until the day of death, and the day of death atones, along with repentance.

VII.1 A. They [immediately, in this world] pay off the reward owing to the wicked [for such good as they may do], while they credit to the righteous [the reward that is coming to them, but do not pay it off, rather paying them off in the world to come].

B. They pay off the reward owing to the wicked [in this world] as though they were people who had carried out the Torah ungrudgingly, in whom no fault had ever been found.

C. They credit to the righteous [the reward that is coming to them, but do not pay it off, rather paying them off in the world to come], as though they were people lacking all good traits.

D.   They thus give a little bit to each party, with the bulk of the remainder laid up for them.

III. Matters of Philosophy, Natural Science and Metaphysics

Nothing of metaphysical interest intrudes.

70

The Fathers According to Rabbi Nathan Chapter Forty

This chapter does not contribute to our study.

71

The Fathers According to
Rabbi Nathan Chapter Forty-One

For our study this chapter is null.

Appendix One

"Judaism beyond the Texts," or "Judaism behind the Texts"? Formulating a Debate

Some scholars just now claim that there is a "Judaism out there," beyond any one document, to which in some way or other all documents in various ways and proportions are supposed to attest. And that Judaism out there, prior to, encompassing all documents, each with its "Judaism in here" imposes its judgment upon our reading of every sentence, every paragraph, every book. A reading of a single document therefore is improper. All documents have to be read in light of all other documents; none sustains a distinctive reading; a hermeneutics serving one explains all the others. This view may be framed in the phrase, "Judaism beyond the texts," which is to say, we have to read the various documents to find evidence of the nurturing, sheltering Judaic system that transcends them all and encompasses each one equally well. To discover that Judaism, we have to identify the premises and presuppositions of documents and their contents, for when we find out what the documents take for granted, we are led into the documentary matrix, which is to say, that Judaism that comes prior to any particular Judaic system, that Judaism to which all Judaisms subscribe.

The contrary view begins with the same question, which is to say, what do we know from a text about its framers' premises and presuppositions? That is precisely the question that precipitates research into the Judaism beyond the texts. But it is answered in a different way, by reason of a different premise. The premise of those who ask presuppositions to tell us about a Judaism beyond a given document is that a text tells us something beyond itself. But those who ask the premises to attest to the inner structure of thought on which a document's details rest insist that a text, inclusive of its premises and presuppositions, attests only to itself: its framers' views, its authors' conceptions. What lies beyond the text we cannot know from any one text, or from all of them put together. Accordingly, research on the character and consequences of the premises of a document will have to turn inward, asking about the Judaism behind the text, the system presupposed by a given document. Let me explain how it came to the fore and what is at stake.

A considerable debate concerning the Judaism supposedly implicit in, and beyond, any given document of that Judaism, presently enlivens all scholarship on the literature of formative Judaism. Specifically, people wonder whether and how we may describe, beyond the evidence of what an authorship has given us in its particular piece of writing, what that authorship knew, had in mind, took for granted, and otherwise affirmed as its larger "Judaism." Nearly fifteen years ago I precipitated matters in my *Judaism: The Evidence of the Mishnah.* Specifically, I proposed to describe the system and structure of a given document and ask what "Judaism" – way of life, worldview, address to a defined "Israel" – emerged from that document. The notion that documents are to be read one by one and not as part of a larger canonical statement – the one whole Torah of Moses, our rabbi, for example – troubled colleagues, and not without reason. For reading the literature, one book at a time, and describing, analyzing, and interpreting the system presented by a document that, to begin with, invited systemic analysis set aside received notions in three ways.

First, as is clear, the conception of the document as part of a prior and encompassing tradition now met competition. Second, I dismissed the prevailing notion that we may describe on the basis of whatever we find in any given document a composite "Judaism" (or some qualification thereof, for example, classical, Rabbinic, Talmudic, normative, what-have-you-Judaism). Third, I treated as merely interesting the received and hitherto commanding tradition of exegesis, imputing to the ancient texts meanings not to be tampered with.

For example, I translated fully half a dozen tractates of the Bavli without referring in any systematic way (or at all) to Rashi's interpretation of a single passage, let alone accepting at face value his reading and sense of the whole. I dismissed as pertinent only to their own times the contributions of later authorships to the description of the Judaism attested by earlier documents. These things I did for good and substantial reason, which Western academic learning has recognized since the Renaissance: the obvious fallacy of anachronism being the compelling and first one, utter gullibility as to assertions of received writings, an obvious second. But, further, I maintain, along with nearly the whole of academic secular learning, that each document derives from a context, and to begin with is to be read in that context and interpreted, at the outset, as a statement of and to a particular setting. Constructs such as -*ism*s and -*ities* come afterward (if they are admitted into discourse at all). Not only so, but in the case of ancient Judaism, a mass of confused and contradictory evidence, deriving from Jews of a broad variety of opinion, requires not harmonization but sorting out. The solution to the disharmonies – a process of theological selection, for example, of what is normative, classical, Talmudic, Rabbinic, or, perhaps, Jewish-Christian, Hellenistic-Jewish, and the like – no longer solved many problems.

From this quest for "the Judaism beyond" the documents, so familiar and so much cherished by the received scholarly and theological tradition, with no regret I took my leave. My absence was soon noticed – and vigorously protested, as is only right and proper in academic discourse. One statement of the matter derives from the British medievalist, Hyam Maccoby:

> Neusner argues that since the Mishnah has its own style and program, nothing outside it is relevant to explaining it. This is an obvious fallacy. The Mishnah, as a digest, in the main, of the legal...aspect of rabbinic Judaism, necessarily has its own style and program. But to treat it as something intended to be a comprehensive compendium of the Oral Torah is simply to beg the question. Neusner does not answer the point, put to him by E. P. Sanders and myself, that the liturgy being presupposed by the Mishnah, is surely relevant to the Mishnah's exegesis. Nor does he answer the charge that he ignores the aggadic material within the Mishnah itself, for example, Abot; or explain why the copious aggadic material found in roughly contemporaneous works should be regarded as irrelevant. Instead he insists that he is right to carry out the highly artificial project of deliberately closing his eyes to all aggadic material, and trying to explain the Mishnah without it.[1]

Maccoby exhibits a somewhat infirm grasp upon the nature of the inquiry before us. If one starts with the question, "What does the authorship of this book mean to say, when read by itself and not in light of other, *later* writings?" then it would be improper to import into the description of the system of the Mishnah in particular (its "Judaism" – hence "Judaism: The evidence of the Mishnah") conceptions not contained within its pages.[2] Tractate Abot, for one instance, cites a range

---

[1]Writing in the symposium, "The Mishnah: Methods of Interpretation," *Midstream*, October, 1986, p. 41. Maccoby's deplorable personal animadversions may be ignored.

[2]I stated explicitly at no fewer than six points in the book my recognition that diverse ideas floated about, and insisted that the authorship of the Mishnah can have entertained such ideas. But the statement that they made in the Mishnah did not contain them, and therefore was to be read without them. Alas, the few

of authorities who lived a generation beyond the closure of the (rest of the) Mishnah and so is ordinarily dated[3] to about 250, with the Mishnah dated to about 200. On that basis how one can impute to the Mishnah's system conceptions first attaining closure half a century later I do not know. To describe the Mishnah, for example, as a part of "Rabbinic Judaism" is to invoke the premise that we know, more or less on its own, just what this "Rabbinic Judaism" is and says.

But what we cannot show we do not know. And, as a matter of established fact, many conceptions dominant in the final statements of Rabbinic Judaism to emerge from late antiquity play no material role whatsoever in the system of the Mishnah, or, for that matter, of Tosefta and Abot. No one who has looked for the conception of "the Oral Torah" in the Mishnah or in the documents that succeeded it, for the next two hundred years, will understand why Maccoby is so certain that the category of Oral Torah, or the myth of the Dual Torah, applies at all. For the mythic category of "Oral Torah" makes its appearance, so far as I can discern, only with the Yerushalmi and not in any document closed prior to that time, although a notion of a revelation over and above Scripture – not called "Oral Torah" to be sure – comes to expression in Abot. Implicitly, moreover, certain sayings of the Mishnah itself, for example, concerning rulings of the Torah and rulings of sages, may contain the notion of a secondary tradition, beyond revelation. But that tradition is not called "the Oral Torah," and I was disappointed to find that even in the Yerushalmi the mythic statement of the matter, so far as I can see, is lacking. It is only in the Bavli, for example, in the famous story of Hillel and Shammai and the convert at b. Shab. 30b-31a, that the matter is fully explicit. Now, if Maccoby maintains that the conception circulated in the form in which we know it, for example, in the Yerushalmi in truncated form or in the Bavli in complete form, he should supply us with the

---

reviews that the book did receive contained no evidence that the reviewers understood that simple, and repeated caveat. Jakob J. Petuchowski in *Religious Studies Review* for July, 1983, subjected the book to a savage attack of trivializing and with vast condescension imputed to the book precisely the opposite of its message, as, we see, does Maccoby.

[3] I take responsibility for not a single date in any writing of mine, culling them all from available encyclopedia articles, in the notion that those articles, e.g., the splendid one by M.D. Heer in *Encyclopaedia Judaica* s.v. *Midrash*, represent the consensus of learning at this time. I do not know why Maccoby and Sanders reject the consensus on Abot, since, to my knowledge, neither of them has published a scholarly article on the dating of the document. But I believe my position accords from what is presently "common knowledge." If it does not, I should rapidly correct it.

evidence for his position.[4] As I said, what we cannot show we do not know. And most secular and academic scholarship concurs that we have no historical knowledge a priori, though in writing Maccoby has indeed in so many words maintained that we do. In fact the documents of formative Judaism do yield histories of ideas, and not every idea can be shown to have taken part in the statement of each, let alone all, of the documents. But those who appeal to a Judaism out there, before and beyond all of the documents, ignore that fact.

Sanders and Maccoby seem more certain of the content of the liturgy than the rest of scholarship, which tends to a certain reserve on the matter of the wording and language of prayer. Maccoby's "roughly contemporaneous" aggadic works cite the Mishnah as a completed document, for example, Sifra and the two Sifrés, and so therefore are to be dated in the period beyond the closure of the Mishnah.[5] Unless we accept at face value the attribution of a saying to the person to whom a document's editorship assigns it, we know only that date of closure for the contents of a document. True, we may attempt to show that a saying derives from a period prior to the closure of a document; but we cannot take for granted that sayings belong to the age and the person in whose name they are given. These are simple truisms of all critical learning, and, once we understand and take them to heart, we find it necessary to do precisely what I have done, which is to read each document first of all on its own and in its framework and terms.[6]

---

[4]Maccoby may not have read my *Torah: From Scroll to Symbol in Formative Judaism* (Philadelphia, 1985: Fortress Press). There I survey the materials that stand behind the statements made here.

[5]I utterly ignore Mekhilta deR. Ishmael, because of the important article by Ben Zion Wacholder on the date of the document, published in 1969 in *Hebrew Union College Annual*. I have not worked on that Mekhilta and have yet to see any scholarly discussion of Wacholder's most interesting arguments in behalf of the view that in Mekhilta deR. Ishmael we deal with what is in fact a medieval document. Not knowing how to sort out the issues, I have simply bypassed the evidence of that document at this time. Wacholder takes for granted that merely because the names of authorities that occur in the Mishnah also occur in Mekhilta deR. Ishmael, we cannot maintain that that writing derives from the period of the Mishnah. Since everyone has known for a half-century that the Zohar, attributed to Tannaite authority, in fact was made up in the high Middle Ages as a work of pseudo-imitation (there is in fact nothing imitative about it), Wacholder surely expressed a kind of consensus. But that consensus has not yet affected the reading of the documents of late antiquity, all sayings of which are assigned to those to whom they are attributed – pure and simple.

[6]Maccoby further seems not to have read a variety of scholarship. He says that it is absurd to say that "the Mishnah is not much concerned with justice, or with repentance, or with the Messiah." He does not seem to realize the way in which the Messiah theme is used in the Mishnah, by contrast to its use in other

At stake are not merely literary, but also cultural and religious conceptions. So let us return to this matter of "the Judaism beyond" to explain the connection between a narrowly hermeneutical debate and the much broader issue of culture and the nature of religion. When I speak of "the Judaism beyond," I mean a conception of a very concrete character. To define by example, I invoke the definition of this "Judaism out there" operative in the mind of E.P. Sanders when Sanders describes rabbinic writings. In my debates with Sanders[7] I have complained that his categories seem to me improperly formed, since the rabbinic texts do not conform to the taxonomy Sanders utilizes. They in other words are not talking about the things Sanders wants them to discuss. That complaint is turned against me, as we see, in Maccoby's critique of my picture of how we may describe (not "explain," as Maccoby would have it) the system of the Mishnah in particular.

Commenting on this debate with Sanders, William Scott Green says, Sanders "reads rabbinic texts by peering through them for the ideas (presumably ones Jews or rabbis believed) that lie beneath them." This runs parallel to Maccoby's criticism of my "ignoring" a variety of conceptions I do not find in the Mishnah. Both Maccoby and Sanders, in my view, wish to discuss what *they* think important – that is, presentable

---

documents, as demonstrated in my *Messiah in Context. Israel's History and Destiny in Formative Judaism* (Philadelphia, 1983: Fortress Press). I am genuinely puzzled at who has said that the Mishnah is not much concerned with justice or with repentance. I look in vain for such statements on the part of any scholar, myself included. Mishnah-tractate Yoma on repentance and Mishnah-tractate Sanhedrin on the institutions of justice have not, to my knowledge, been ignored in my account of the Mishnah and its literature and system. It would appear that Maccoby reads somewhat selectively.

[7]These begin in my review of his *Paul and Palestinian Judaism*, in *History of Religion* 1978, 18:177-191. I reprinted the review in my *Ancient Judaism: Debates and Disputes* (Chico, 1984: Scholars Press for Brown Judaic Studies), where I review more than a score of modern and contemporary books in the field in which I work and also present several bibliographic essays and state-of-the-question studies. I also reworked parts of my Sanders review in essays on other problems. To my knowledge he has not reviewed my *Judaism: The Evidence of the Mishnah*, and if he has in print responded to my questions of method addressed to his *Paul and Palestinian Judaism*, I cannot say where he has done so. Quite to the contrary, in his *Paul, The Law, and the Jewish People* (Philadelphia, 1985: Fortress), which I review also in my *Ancient Judaism*, where he claims to reply to critics of the original book, he not only ignores my review, and also that of Anthony J. Saldarini in *Journal of Biblical Literature*, cited in my review of *Paul, The Law, and the Jewish People*, which makes the same point, but he even omits from his list of reviews of the original work Saldarini's review as well as mine. This seems to me to impede scholarly debate.

in terms of contemporary religious disputation[8] – and therefore to ignore what the texts themselves actually talk about, as Green says, "the materials that attracted the attention and interest of the writers."[9] In my original review I pointed out that Sanders's categories ignore what the texts actually say and impose categories the Judaic-rabbinic texts do not know. Sanders, in Green's judgment, introduces a distinct premise:

> For Sanders, the religion of Mishnah lies unspoken beneath its surface; for Neusner it is manifest in Mishnah's own language and preoccupations.[10]

Generalizing on this case, Green further comments in those more general terms that bring us into a debate on the nature of religion and culture, and that larger discourse lends importance to what, in other circumstances, looks to be a mere academic argument. Green writes as follows:

> The basic attitude of mind characteristic of the study of religion holds that religion is certainly in your soul, likely in your heart, perhaps in your mind, but never in your body. That attitude encourages us to construe religion cerebrally and individually, to think in terms of beliefs and the believer, rather than in terms of behavior and community. The lens provided by this prejudice draws our attention to the intense and obsessive belief called "faith," so religion is understood as a state of mind, the object of intellectual or emotional commitment, the result of decisions to believe or to have faith. According to this model, people

---

[8]Maccoby makes this explicit in his contribution to the symposium cited above, "The Mishnah: Methods of Interpretation," *Midstream,* October, 1986, p. 41, "It leads to Neusner's endorsement of 19th-century German anti-Jewish scholarship.... [Neusner] admires the Mishnah for the very things that the New Testament alleges against the Pharisees: for formalism, attention to petty legalistic detail, and for a structuralist patterning of reality in terms of 'holiness' rather than of morality, justice, and love of neighbor." Here Maccoby introduces the bias of Reform Judaism, with its indifference to "petty legalistic detail." But I (among millions of Jews) find intensely meaningful the holy way of life embodied, for one example, in concern for what I eat for breakfast, along with love of neighbor, and the conception that the Judaic way of life leads to a realm of holiness is hardly my invention. It is contained in the formula of the blessing, *...who has sanctified us by the commandments and commanded us to....* I can treat with respect Maccoby's wish to describe as his Judaism some other system than the received one, but the "very things" that the New Testament alleges against the Pharisees are recapitulated by the Reform critique of the way of life of the Judaism of the Dual Torah, today embodied in Orthodoxy and Conservative Judaism, to which I adhere. It follows that not all of the "other side" are Orthodox, although, as to intertextuality, that seems to be the sector from which the principal advocates derive.

[9] Personal letter, January 17, 1985.

[10]William Scott Green in his Introduction, *Approaches to Ancient Judaism* (Chicago, 1980: Scholars Press for Brown Judaic Studies) II, p. xxi.

have religion but they do not do their religion. Thus we tend to devalue behavior and performance, to make it epiphenomenal, and of course to emphasize thinking and reflecting, the practice of theology, as a primary activity of religious people.... The famous slogan that "ritual recapitulates myth" follows this model by assigning priority to the story and to peoples' believing the story, and makes behavior simply an imitation, an aping, a mere acting out.[11]

Now as we reflect on Green's observations, we of course recognize what is at stake. It is the definition of religion, or, rather, what matters in or about religion, emerging from one reading of Protestant theology and Protestant religious experience.

For when we lay heavy emphasis on faith to the exclusion of works, on the individual rather than on society, on conscience instead of culture, and when, as in the language of Maccoby, we treat behavior and performance by groups as less important, and present as more important the matters of thinking, reflecting, theology and belief – not to mention the abstractions of "love of neighbor" and "morality," to which Reform theologians in the pattern of Maccoby adhere, we simply adopt as normative for academic scholarship convictions critical to the Lutheran wing of the Protestant Reformation. And that accounts for the absolutely accurate instinct of Maccoby in introducing into the debate the positions of the Lutheran New Testament scholars who have dominated New Testament scholarship in Germany and the United States (but not Britain or France).

Judaism and the historical, classical forms of historical Christianity, Roman Catholic and Orthodox, as well as important elements of the Protestant Reformation, however, place emphasis on religion as a matter of works and not faith alone, behavior and community as well as belief and conscience. Religion is something that people do, and they do it together. Religion is not something people merely have, as individuals. Since the entire civilization of the West, from the fourth century onward, has carried forward the convictions of Christianity, not about the individual alone but about politics and culture, we may hardly find surprising the Roman Catholic conviction that religion flourishes not alone in heart and mind, but in eternal social forms: the Church, in former times, the state as well.

At stake in the present debate therefore is the fundamental issue of hermeneutics. For claims as to the character of the literature of Judaism entail judgments on the correct hermeneutics, down to the interpretation of words and phrases. We can read everything only in light of everything else, fore and aft. That is how today nearly everyone

---

[11]Personal letter, January 17, 1985.

interested in these writings claims to read them – citing the Bavli as proof for that hermeneutics. Or we can read each item first of all on its own, a document as an autonomous and cogent and utterly rational, syllogistic statement, a unit of discourse as a complete and whole composition, entire unto itself, taking account, to be sure, of how, in the larger context imposed from without, meanings change(d). That is how – and not solely on the basis of the sample we have surveyed – I maintain any writing must be read: in its own context, entirely on its own, not only in the one imposed by the audience and community that preserved it.

For whatever happens to thought, in the mind of the thinker ideas come to birth cogent, whole, complete – and on their own. Extrinsic considerations of context and circumstance play their role, but logic, cogent discourse, rhetoric – these enjoy an existence, an integrity, too. If sentences bear meaning on their own, then to insist that sentences bear meaning only in line with friends, companions, partners in meaning contradicts the inner logic of syntax that, on its own, imparts sense to sentences. These are the choices: everything imputed, as against an inner integrity of logic and the syntax of syllogistic thought.[12] But there is no compromise between what I argue is the theologically grounded hermeneutic, taken as a given by diverse believers, and the descriptive and historical, utterly secular hermeneutic which I advocate. As between the philosophical heritage of Athens and any other hermeneutics, I maintain that "our sages of blessed memory" demonstrate the power of the philosophical reading of the one whole Torah of Moses, our rabbi. And, further, I should propose that the reason for our sages' remarkable success in persuading successive generations of Israel of the Torah's ineluctable truth lies not in arguments from tradition, from "Sinai," so much as in appeals to the self-evidence of the well-framed argument, the well-crafted sentence of thought.

If the mythic appeal stands for religion, and the reasoned position for secularity, then I point to what in Judaism we call "our sages of blessed memory," masters of the one whole Torah of Moses, our rabbi, as paragons of practical logic and secular reason. Why at the end introduce the (inflammatory, provocative) category of secularity? The reason is that the literature of Judaism, exemplified by the Bavli, commonly finds representation as wholly continuous, so that everything always testifies to the meaning of everything else, and, moreover, no book demands or

---

[12]No one can maintain that the meanings of words and phrases, the uses of syntax, bear meanings wholly integral to discrete occasions. Syntax works because it joins mind to mind, and no mind invents language. But that begs the question and may be dismissed as impertinent, since the contrary view claims far more than the social foundation of the language.

sustains a reading on its own. As a theological judgment, that (religious) view enjoys self-evidence, since, after all, "Judaism" is a "religion," and it presents its doctrines and dogmas, rules and regulations. So every document contributes to that one and encompassing system, that Judaism. But a system, a religion, makes its judgments at the end, post facto, while the authorships at hand worked at the outset, de novo. They were philosophers in the deepest and richest sense of the tradition of philosophy. In that sense (but that sense alone) I classify our sages as fundamentally secular. I mean to say that a secular hermeneutics for a theological literature alone can lead us to learn how to read their writing. The upshot of such a hermeneutics can only be a profoundly reasoned, religious view of a rational and well-proportioned world: a world of rules and order and reason and rationality. That constitutes their religion: the affirmation of creation as a work of logic and order and law, to which the human mind, with its sense of logic, order, and rule, conforms, as it was created to conform.

So reading what they wrote – a problem of textual analysis and interpretation – undergoes distortion of we impose, to begin with, the after-the-fact interpretation of the audience that received the writing. We err if we confuse social and theological with literary and hermeneutical categories, and the religious system at the end constitutes a social and theological, not a literary classification. Hermeneutics begins within the text and cannot sustain definition on the basis of the (later, extrinsic) disposition of the text. Nor should we miss the gross anachronism represented by the view that the way things came out all together at the end imposes its meaning and character upon the way things started out, one by one. Reading the Mishnah, ca. 200, as the framers of the two Talmuds read it two hundred, then four hundred years later, vastly distorts the original document in its own setting and meaning – and that by definition. But the same must be said, we now see, of the Bavli: reading the Bavli as if any other authorship but the Bavli's authorship played a part in making the statement of the Bavli is simply an error.[13] A

---

[13]Critics of my translations of the Bavli into English prove the necessity of making this simple point, because they invariably fault me for translating not in accord with the medieval interpreter, Solomon Isaac (1040-1105), "Rashi." They accuse me not of ignoring Rashi, to which I plead guilty, but not understanding Rashi. But I consistently translate the words before me, as best I can, without reference to Rashi's interpretation of them – except – for reason, not for piety – as an interesting possibility. I point to the world of biblical scholarship, which manages to translate the Hebrew Scriptures without consistently accepting the interpretation of the medieval commentators. Why should the Talmuds be treated differently? There are other approaches to the sense and meaning, other

mark of the primitive character of discourse[14] in the field at hand derives from the need to point to self-evident anachronism in the prevailing hermeneutics.

---

criteria, other definitions of the problem. But we cannot expect a hearing from those who know in advance that Rashi has said the last word on the matter.

[14]We note that Shaye Cohen is explicit about indifference to priority or documents.

Appendix Two

The Talmudic-Midrashic View of...:
A Current Exemplification of an
Old Error in Scholarship

Samuel Tobias Lachs, *Humanism in Talmud and Midrash*
(Rutherford, 1992: Fairleigh Dickinson University Press), 150 pp.

Professor Samuel Tobias Lachs, Bryn Mawr College, announces as
his purpose the collection and arrangement of passages "in the Talmud
and midrash" that "reflect an anthropocentric, rather than a theocentric
view of the world." The passages are arranged topically, "to illustrate
how some of the rabbis of the talmudic era subscribed to a view of the
world which starts with man rather than with God and is reflected in
their observations about the human condition." No one has done so
before, he says, because, he thinks, "it is the result of theological
cowardice, motivated by a fear that by assembling the data in a logical
order, and examining them separately, more traditional theological
approaches might be compromised or rejected." But, as we shall see,
Lachs announces a distinction that makes no difference at all. That is,
first, because he proposes to disprove a proposition nobody holds; and
second, because he ignores all of the rules of professional scholarship.

To accomplish his stated goal, Lachs begins with an introduction, in
which he explains that "the early rabbis gradually wrested the Torah and
the right to its interpretation from this absolute and autocratic control of
the priesthood," which they replaced: "the priesthood was not the
favored institution of many of the rabbis because of its clerical nature,
which was antithetical to their egalitarian view of society." The
prophets, too, were succeeded by these same rabbis "as the moral
conscience of the people." Lachs explains, "The prophetic movement
came to an end once the people had direct access to the Torah." That

brings Lachs to "the transmission of tradition from the prophets directly to the men of the Great Synagogue." So the rabbis assumed "three traditional roles...from their biblical predecessors." After this exercise in pseudo-history – not a sentence in his account stands on the critical foundations of scholarship as it is practiced today! – he reaches his topic.

"Theocentrism" is contrasted with "a strong anthropocentric orientation." The legacy of priest and prophet is "theocentric," but the sage's legacy – that of the Old Testament Wisdom literature is what he means – is "anthropocentric." Theocentrism dominated because "man stands in awe of authority;" "the Torah describes its own divine character and provenance, [so] the theocentric outlook would naturally prevail;" and "religion by its very nature is conservative. Sacred texts deemed divine in origin are said not to change.... The theocentrist almost always tends to be a strict constructionist of the Law...." What is bothering him, therefore, is not theology at all, but attitudes toward the law and tradition; his "theocentrists" really are conservative, and his "humanists," not so; so the fight is between Orthodox and Conservative Judaism in eastern Pennsylvania as Lachs wishes to frame matters.

His Conservative Judaism enters when he maintains,

> There were those who would not be resigned to intellectual inertia nor intimidated by the thought of change.... It is precisely because of their commitment to free inquiry and this ordering of priorities that illustrates their choice of the anthropocentric over the theocentric view of the world. They deeply respected tradition, but would not permit it to immobilize them either in thought or in action. Because they questioned it and subjected it to rational inquiry they represented a healthy challenge to the comfortable stability of the exponents of an authoritative, revealed tradition.

Lachs proceeds to persuade himself that he has correctly characterized Rabbinic Judaism in maintaining that it is, in his categories, "anthropocentric," and not "theocentric." It follows that his categories are wildly out of kilter, since his discussion concerns not theology but the politics of traditional Judaism in the United States. That is not to suggest he ever comes to the point. His anthology ,merely meanders through these categories: man and society; God; Torah; and divine revelation and human authorship. Each of the chapters consists of strung together allusions to various passages, none of them cited or analyzed, so readers are left to believe, or disbelieve, Lachs's paraphrase and allegations as to the sense and meaning of the passages.

Lachs's polemic is that of a Conservative rabbi against Orthodox Judaism, since it is difficult to identify anyone else who to begin with might take seriously what has provoked his "research." Precisely what it means to "start with man" rather than "with God" he really does not spell out with any clarity; he seems to know that everyone agrees on the sense and importance of what he is trying to prove, and to grasp what is at stake. That, of course, is plausible only in the circle of true believers in the method and proposition at hand. Since Reform Judaism rarely constructs theological arguments on the strength of the Rabbinic documents alone, and since Orthodox Judaism in its various formulations and versions forms the butt of Lachs's polemic, Conservative Judaism – meaning, a handful of Orthodox rabbis serving Reform congregations – remains as the beneficiary.

Lachs claims that where our sages of blessed memory show respect for rigorous argument and reason, they are among his "humanists." But then the whole of Rabbinic Judaism conforms to his prescription, since, after all, there is no more rational or elegantly and rigorously argued piece of writing in world literature than the Talmud of Babylonia. That is a monument to the conviction of our sages of blessed memory that the human mind is in the model, "in our image, after our likeness," of the mind of God, made manifest through the Torah. So, as they say, "iqqar haser min hassefer," the book forgets its main point! The stated proposition is pure gibberish. "Our sages of blessed memory" believed in a supernatural God, whom they encountered in the Torah. Everybody knows that. What it means, then, to distinguish "starting with God" from "starting with man" is not at all obvious, except to Lachs.

But it is not the substance of matters that marks the book as an exercise in confused babble. What is wrong with this book is that it contains not a single well-argued, clearly formulated, and rigorously demonstrated proposition. A person may be guilty of "publishing too much" by publishing a single book, if it lacks a fresh and important idea. And this kind of neo-primitivism – a cro-Magnon hunting and gathering, a puerile collecting and arranging – can scarcely claim to propose any ideas at all. I am inclined to think that Lachs is obscure on that matter because he is just babbling. In fact, he has set up for himself some sort of straw man, whom it is easy to knock down. The chapters that form the shank of the book are filled with a kind of stream-of-consciousness free association. I could cite hundreds of paragraphs to illustrate the pointlessness of the run-on babble, but none would convey the flavor of the whole.

Lachs knows nothing of a vast literature of history and theology devoted to each of the topics of his chapters. That fact is proven in a very simple way. Examine his footnotes. Nearly all of them consist of brief allusions to sources; in any fifty footnotes, he cites scarcely a single monographic work, one that has covered the same sources, the same problems, the same issues. Reinventing the wheel, Lachs deliberately obscures the fact that he is not the first to take up the themes at hand.

Then, too, readers are unlikely to know that his book represents a huge step backward, into an age in which "scholarship" on Judaism consisted of collecting this and that and passing one's opinion. Studies on such and so an idea "in Talmud and Midrash," lacking historical precision, documentary concreteness, and philosophical clarity, no longer are published in English, since the scholarly world no longer tolerates this kind of amateurism. Standards have risen; expectations are higher; making things up as you go along and publishing the result no longer suffices. This is not a work of scholarship, it is an act of contempt for scholarship.

It also is not a work of argument for a broad audience, since the writing is obscure and allusive, not clear and focused. I cannot imagine a nonspecialist audience for a sentence such as this (among thousands): "As the rabbis rejected Greco-Roman gnosticism and its dualistic theology so, too, they rejected and opposed the Christian concept of an antagonistic dichotomy in man." As a matter of fact, without a Ph.D. in the history of religion, readers are unlikely to know what he is talking about. And they also are not apt to realize that his characterization of "the rabbis" is challenged in study after study, beginning after all with Scholem, on the one side, or that his portrait of "Christian concept" is one that will amaze, for its ignorance, a vast number of historians of Christian thought, who can cite chapter and verse of Church Fathers' writings to contradict his monolithic description of what was a highly complex and variegated set of Christian systems. Not many people any more imagine a single "Christianity" to match a single "the rabbis...."

This is, as I said, just a case of publishing a book even though the author has nothing to say in the book: hunting and gathering, collecting and arranging – and then a whole lot of free-association and fabrication. Lachs has published only two books but provides a fine example of publishing too much, since his *Rabbinic Commentary on the New Testament* (1987) exhibits the same intellectual incompetence. There he collects and arranges passages he thinks relevant to various Gospels' passages and then passes his opinion on this and that; there, too, he cites only a tiny fraction of the existing literature of the same sort; there, too, he thinks hunting and gathering, collecting and arranging, is learning. And most of the reviews of that worthless exercise said exactly that.

I assume lots of Conservative synagogues will want this party platform for their libraries, even though their members are unlikely to read it. But apart from that trivial audience, the book will quickly find its way into the bowels of research libraries, which buy everything automatically, and then languish, as it should. It neither informs, nor challenges, nor makes an important argument, nor argues an intelligible thesis: it is a book that did not have to be written, the sort of which our

Israeli colleagues say, "Pity the trees" (cut down to make the paper to print the book...).

Appendix Three

The Diversity of Rabbinic Documents and Their Premises

A Case in Point: Why Do Rabbinic Authors Cite Sayings in the Name of Particular Sages?

Since this inquiry concerns the premises and presuppositions of documents, it is important that we take account of a variety of givens that our survey by its nature misses. I refer to points that documents never articulate at all but that, upon closer inspection, prove quite distinctive to one writing or another. Here we see that, if we look at matters from a distance, everything looks alike, but when we take up the documents one by one, the writings turn out to differ from one another at their deepest layers of composition and construction. What the facts that I shall now set forth mean for our inquiry into the Judaism behind the texts is self-evident. We may never take for granted that what one text takes as its premise, all other texts accept as well. Documents must be read one by one, and only when we have identified the characteristic traits of each may we proceed to ask how documents form a common corpus, either a canon of writing or a corpus of shared convictions.

To demonstrate the profoundly distinctive traits of each writing, I take up a simple question: Why do various compilations attribute sayings to named authorities, as is the simple fact? Can we give a single answer to that question, or do the various documents utilize for diverse and even contradictory purposes the attributions of sayings to named authorities? I shall show that each of four documents, the Mishnah,

Tractate Abot, the Tosefta, and the Talmud of the Land of Israel, makes use in its own way of the attribution of sayings to specific persons. What one compilation signals by attributions another cannot concede, and what the other means to say through attributions the one cannot grasp. Any effort to harmonize the premises yielded by the appeal to attributions then requires us to hold together contradictory sayings, therefore to misunderstand and misinterpret the data before us.

To understand the issue at hand we have to take account of two contradictory facts. First, all rabbinic documents are anonymous, and all of them include vast numbers of compositions bearing no assignments; none of the compositions of which a document is comprised is assigned to a named author; no document bears a dependable attribution to a specific person. But, by way of contradiction to these facts, every one of the documents of the Judaism of the Dual Torah produced in the formative age is characterized by numerous attributions of statements to specific figures. So individuals at the same time play no role and also dominate the representation of discourse. The literary situation is characterized by William Green in the following way:

> Most rabbinic documents are unattributed works; all in fact are anonymous.... Rabbinic literature has no authors. No document claims to be the writing of an individual rabbi in his own words; and all contain the ostensible sayings of, and stories about, many rabbis, usually of several generations. Selected to suit the purposes of compilers and redactors, the documents' components are not pristine and natural. They have been revised and reformulated in the processes of transmission and redaction, with the consequence that the ipsissima verba of any rabbis are beyond recovery. Rabbinic literature is severely edited, anonymous, and collective.[1]

These contradictory traits – exclusion of distinctive, personal traits of style, absolute refusal to recognize an individual in his own setting, for example, by preserving a book written by, or about, a named authority, and, at the same time, ubiquitous and persistent inclusion of names along with sayings – provoke the question at hand. If the literature were anonymous as well as collective, or if it exhibited the marks of individuality along with its constant references to named figures, we should not find puzzling the definitive trait before us. So to the work at hand.

The question is addressed to me, "Why is the rabbinic literature so interested in coupling utterances and decisions with names?" The question finds a facile answer for those who take for granted that issues

---

[1]William Scott Green, "Storytelling and Holy Men," in J. Neusner, ed., *Take Judaism, For Example. Studies toward the Comparison of Religions* (Atlanta, 1992: Scholars Press for South Florida Studies in the History of Judaism), p. 30.

of history govern in the formulation of the Judaism of the Dual Torah. If the primary interest lies in what really happened, so that events of a specific, one-time character bear incontrovertible and compelling truth, then names are attached to sayings to indicate who really said them; then the word "really" carries the meaning, which particular authority stands behind a given statement? That premise, at the same time historical and biographical, certainly has much to recommend it, since, in our culture, with its two-century-old stress on the authority of demonstrable, historical fact, if we can show that something really happened or was truly said by the person to whom it is attributed, then much else follows. But for our sages of blessed memory, particularly in the two Talmuds, that premise will have presented considerable difficulty.

For we look in vain in the analytical documents for evidence to sustain the stated premise that people really concerned themselves with the issue of who really said what. That is to say, while sayings are attributed, the purpose of the attribution – what is at stake in it, what else we know because we know it – requires analysis in its own terms. Since, as a matter of fact, a saying assigned to one authority in document A will circulate in the name of another in document B, the one-time, determinate assignment of said saying to authority X rather than authority Y cannot be accorded enormous consequence. If the documents were broadly circulated and known, then people ought to have observed that a given saying is assigned to more than a single authority and ought also to have asked why that was the fact. But discussion on that question no where takes a central position in the literature. It is no more troublesome than the fact that a given authority will be assigned a given saying in two or more contexts; then, as with the Sermon on the Mount and the Sermon on the Plain, people will simply maintain (as do the true believers in the historicity of everything in the rabbinic literature who dominate scholarly discourse in the Israeli universities and the Western yeshivot and seminaries), "he would often say...," or, "many times he said...."

Where, when, and why, then, do the names of authorities play a consequential role in the unfolding of discourse? What role is assigned to them, and what premises seem to underpin the constant citation of sayings in the names of particular masters? To answer these questions, it will hardly suffice to speculate. Our task is to turn to the documents themselves and to ask the broad question, what role do named sages play in these compilations, and on what account do specific names joined with particular statements come under discussion? That question, of course, forms a particular detail of a broader issue, which is, how come specific sages play so critical a role in the rabbinic literature?

When we consider counterpart writings in Christian circles, by contrast, we find a very different kind of writing. There, very commonly, a named figure, whether Matthew or Paul, presents a piece of writing, and he bears responsibility for everything in that document, either as an account of what he has seen and heard, as in the case of Matthew's Gospel, or as an account of his own systematic views, as in the case of Paul's letters. True, we find anonymous writings; but such documents as Hebrews, which bears no named author, also contains no sayings assigned to specific authorities. The much later Zoroastrian law codes, which intersect in contents and at some points even in form with the Judaic ones, assign a given code to a named authority. So we should regard as emblematic and enormously consequential the constant intrusion of the names of authorities in the rabbinic writings, beginning to end, from the Mishnah through the Bavli.

I. The Use of Attributions in the Mishnah: The Claim of Mishnah-tractate Eduyyot

Rather than address the question in general terms, let us first ask about the role of attributions in some few specific documents: How seriously are they taken, and for what purpose? The first document, of course, is the Mishnah. There we find a principal and constitutive form, the dispute, built around the name of opposing authorities, for example, the Houses of Shammai and Hillel, or Aqiba and Tarfon, or Meir and Judah, and the like. We also find in some few passages clear evidence of the collection of statements on a given, cogent problem in the name of a specific authority, for example, Mishnah-tractate Kelim Chapter Twenty-Four is a statement of Judah's views. But, over all, the Mishnah must be described as an entirely anonymous document, which at the same time contains extensive citations of named figures. The same names occur throughout; we cannot demonstrate that a given authority was viewed as particularly knowledgeable in a specific area of law, most of the sages being treated as generalists. At the same time that names predominate everywhere, 62 of the 63 tractates are organized around not named figures but topics, and, as indicated, perhaps 98 percent of the chapters of which those tractates are made up likewise focus on subjects, not named authorities. Only Tractate Eduyyot as a whole is set up around names.

If we turn to that tractate devoted to not a particular subject or problem but rather the collection of attributed sayings and stories told about authorities, what do we find? The answer is, collections of rules on diverse topics, united by the names of authorities cited therein, either disputes, for example, between Shammai and Hillel and their Houses, or sets of rulings representative of a single authority. A single representative passage shows how the document does its work:

1:2   A.   Shammai says, "[Dough which is made] from a qab [of flour is liable] to a dough-offering [Num. 15:20]."

       B.   And Hillel says, "[Dough made] from two qabs."

       C.   And sages say, "It is not in accord with the opinion of this party nor in accord with the opinion of that party,

       D.   "but: [dough made] from a qab and a half of flour is liable to the dough-offering."

Now what is interesting here – and not characteristic of the document throughout – is the inclusion of a final ruling on the dispute, which is different from the rulings of the Houses' founders. That pattern being repeated and so shown to be definitive of the redactor's subtext, the question is raised: Why record not only the official rule, but the opinion of a named, therefore schismatic figure as well? And that of course forms the heart of the matter and tells us the document's answer to our question. First let us consider the source, then draw the conclusion it makes possible:

1:5   A.   And why do they record the opinion of an individual along with that of the majority, since the law follows the opinion of the majority?

       B.   So that, if a court should prefer the opinion of the individual, it may decide to rely upon it.

       C.   For a court has not got the power to nullify the opinion of another court unless it is greater than it in wisdom and in numbers.

       D.   [If] it was greater than the other in wisdom but not in numbers,

       E.   in numbers but not in wisdom,

       F.   it has not got the power to nullify its opinion –

       G.   unless it is greater than it in both wisdom and numbers.

1:6   A.   Said R. Judah, "If so, why do they record the opinion of an individual against that of a majority to no purpose?

       B.   "So that if a person should say, 'Thus have I received the tradition,' one may say to him, 'You have heard the tradition in accord with the opinion of Mr. So-and-so [against that of the majority].'"

The premise of this passage is simple. The law follows the position of the anonymously formulated rule. Then why attribute a rule to a named figure? It is to identify the opinion that is not authoritative, but, nonetheless, subject to consideration. Then it follows, the purpose of citing sayings in the names of authorities is to mark those positions as schismatic and not authoritative – not to validate, but to invalidate.

To test this surmise, we turn to the Tosefta's commentary on the passage of Mishnah-tractate Eduyyot that is before us. Here we find explicitly articulated the premise I identified:

1:4   A.   Under all circumstances the law follows the majority, and the opinion of the individual is recorded along with that of the majority only so as to nullify it.

        B.   R. Judah says, "The opinion of an individual is recorded along with that of the majority only so that, if the times necessitate it, they may rely upon [the opinion of the individual]" [cf. M. Ed. 1:5B].

        C.   And sages say, "The opinion of the individual is recorded along with that of the majority only so that, if later on, this one says, 'Unclean,' and that one says, 'Clean,' one may respond that the one who says it is unclean is in accord with the opinion of R. Eliezer [and the law must follow the majority, which opposed his opinion], so they say to him, 'You have heard this opinion in accord with the ruling of R. Eliezer.'"

Judah's theory of matters – that of the minority – is that the minority opinion registers, so that, under duress, it may serve as precedent; sages take the view that the very opposite consideration pertains; once an opinion is attributed to an individual, that opinion is to be dismissed as schismatic wherever it occurs – even when not in the name of the individual. So we find here confirmation of the surmise that at stake in assigning opinions to names is the formulation of the legal process in such a way as to permit reliable decisions to be made.

But there is a second consideration important to the Mishnah, and that emerges in another passage in the same tractate:

5:6   A.   Aqabia b. Mahalalel gave testimony in four matters.

        B.   They said to him, "Aqabia, retract the four rulings which you laid down, and we shall make you patriarch of the court of Israel."

        C.   He said to them, "It is better for me to be called a fool my whole life but not be deemed a wicked person before the Omnipresent for even one minute,

        D.   "so that people should not say, 'Because he craved after high office, he retracted.'"

The passage proceeds to specify the disputes, and then the narrative continues, reporting that because he refused to retract, sages excommunicated him:

        M.   They excommunicated him, and he died while he was subject to the excommunication, so the court stoned his bier....

5:7   A.   When he was dying, he said to his son, "My son, retract the four rulings which I had laid down."

        B.   He said to him, "And why do you retract now?"

        C.   He said to him, "I heard the rulings in the name of the majority, and they heard them in the name of the majority, so I stood my ground on the tradition which I had heard, and they stood their ground on the tradition they had heard.

        D.   "But you have heard the matter both in the name of an individual and in the name of the majority.

E. "It is better to abandon the opinion of the individual and to hold with the opinion of the majority."

F. He said to him, "Father, give instructions concerning me to your colleagues."

G. He said to him, "I will give no instructions."

H. He said to him, "Is it possible that you have found some fault with me?"

I. He said to him, "No. It is your deeds which will bring you near, or your deeds which will put you off [from the others]."

The crux of the matter then comes at 5:7C: Aqabia has received rulings in the name of the majority and therefore regards them as valid. So the purpose of assigning names to sayings once more is to label the unreliable ones: those in the names of individuals. And at stake, underneath, is of course the shape and structure of the tradition, which is once more stated explicitly: "I stood my ground on the tradition that I had heard...." What comes down anonymously is tradition – from Sinai, obviously – and what bears a name is other than tradition. But matters we see also prove subject to negotiation. Sages bear the obligation to remember what they heard in the name of the majority but also in the name of individuals. So the inclusion of names forms part of a larger theory of tradition and how to be guided by tradition, and the Mishnah's account of itself makes that point in so many words.

II. The Meaning of Attributions to Tractate Abot

We hardly need to find that fact surprising, since the Mishnah's first apologetic, Pirqé Abot, the sayings of the fathers, points to Sinai as the origin of the Mishnah's tradition when it formulates its opening chapter. Tractate Abot in its opening chapter responds to the question: What is the Mishnah? Why should we obey its rules? How does it relate to the Torah, which, we all know, God gave to Israel through Moses at Sinai? The answer is contained in the opening sentence:

The Sayings of the Fathers Chapter One

1:1 Moses received the Torah at Sinai and handed it on to Joshua, Joshua to elders, and elders to prophets. And prophets handed it on to the men of the great assembly. They said three things: Be prudent in judgment. Raise up many disciples. Make a fence for the Torah.

What is important here is three facts. First, the verbs, receive...hand on..., in Hebrew yield the words *qabbalah*, tradition, and *masoret*, also tradition. There is no more lucid or powerful way of making the statement than that: the Torah is a matter of tradition. Second, the tradition goes from master to disciple, Moses to Joshua. So the tradition is not something written down, it is something that lives. Third, we know that the tradition is distinct from the Written Torah, because what is attributed to "the men of the great assembly" (and we have no interest in who these might be assumed to have been) are three statements that do not occur in Scripture. In fact, among all of the sayings in the entire tractate, only very rarely is there attributed to a sage who stands in this chain of tradition a verse of Scripture. So the essence of "the tradition" is not what is said, for example, citing a verse of Scripture and expanding on it, but that a saying is said and who does the saying: a master to a disciple, forward through all time, backward to Sinai. Torah – revelation – stands for a process of transmitting God's will. That process is open-ended but it also is highly disciplined.

How is the question of the origin and authority of the Mishnah answered? The chain of tradition from Sinai ends up with names that are prominent in the Mishnah itself, for example, Shammai and Hillel, and their disciples, the House of Shammai and the House of Hillel. So the message is blatant: major authorities of the Mishnah stand in a chain of tradition to Sinai; hence, the Mishnah contains the Torah of Sinai. It is that straightforward: through discipleship, we reach backward; through the teaching of the sage, we reach forward; the great tradition endures in the learning of the ages. It follows that when sayings are assigned to sages, a quite separate issue is in play. I cite only a small sample of the opening chapter of Abot, which suffices to make my point:

1:2   Simeon the Righteous was one of the last survivors of the great assembly. He would say: On three things does the world stand: On the Torah, and on the Temple service, and on deeds of loving kindness.

1:3   Antigonus of Sokho received [the Torah] from Simeon the Righteous. He would say: Do not be like servants who serve the master on condition of receiving a reward, but [be] like servants who serve the master not on condition of receiving a reward. And let the fear of heaven be upon you.

1:4   Yosé ben Yoezer of Zeredah and Yosé ben Yohanan of Jerusalem received [the Torah] from them. Yosé ben Yoezer says: Let your house be a gathering place for sages. And wallow in the dust of their feet, and drink in their words with gusto.

1:5   Yosé ben Yohanan of Jerusalem says: Let your house be open wide. And seat the poor at your table ["make the poor members of your household"]. And don't talk too much with women. (He referred to a man's wife, all the more so is the rule to be applied to the wife of one's fellow. In this regard did sages say: So long as a man talks too much with a woman, he brings trouble on himself, wastes time better spent on studying the Torah, and ends up an heir of Gehenna.)...

1:12   Hillel and Shammai received [the Torah] from them. Hillel says: Be disciples of Aaron, loving peace and pursuing grace, loving people and drawing them near to the Torah.

1:15 Shammai says: Make your learning of the Torah a fixed obligation. Say little and do much. Greet everybody cheerfully.

1:16 Rabban Gamaliel says: Set up a master for yourself. Avoid doubt. Don't tithe by too much guesswork.

1:17 Simeon his son says: All my life I grew up among the sages, and I found nothing better for a person [the body] than silence. And not the learning is the thing, but the doing. And whoever talks too much causes sin.

1:18 Rabban Simeon ben Gamaliel says: On three things does the world stand: on justice, on truth, and on peace. As it is said, Execute the judgment of truth and peace in your gates. (Zech. 8:16)

Now the key point comes with the beginning of the Mishnah sages themselves, and that is with the pairs, five sets. What is important in this list is the pairs of names and how they are arranged:

Moses
Joshua
Elders
Prophets
Men of the Great Assembly
Simeon the Righteous
Antigonus of Sokho

1.	Yosé ben Yoezer	Yosé b. Yohanan
2.	Joshua b. Perahyah	Nittai the Arbelite
3.	Judah b. Tabbai	Simeon b. Shetah
4.	Shemaiah	Abtalyon
5.	Hillel	Shammai

Gamaliel
Simeon his son
Rabban Simeon b. Gamaliel

The numbered list carries us deep into the pages of the Mishnah itself. But there is another point not to be missed. Once the pairs end, whom do we find? Gamaliel, who is (later on) represented as the son of Hillel, and then Gamaliel and Simeon, his son, Hillel's grandson. The names Gamaliel, then Simeon, continued through this same family, of primary authorities, through Gamaliel II, ruler of the Jewish community after the destruction of the second Temple in 70 and into the second century, then his son, Simeon b. Gamaliel, ruler of the Jewish community after the defeat of Bar Kokhba in 135 – and also, as it happens, the father of Judah the Patriarch, this same Judah the Patriarch who sponsored the Mishnah. So Judah the Patriarch stands in the chain of tradition to Sinai. Not only the teachings of the sages of the Mishnah, but also the political sponsor of the document, who also was numbered among the sages, formed part of this same tradition. What the sages say in these sayings in no way contradicts anything we find in Scripture. But most of what is before us also does not intersect with much that we find in Scripture.

We see, then, two distinct but closely related considerations that operate in the persistent interest in assigning sayings to named authorities. Identifying an authority serves as a taxic indicator of the standing of a saying – classified as not authoritative; but identifying an authority bears the – both correlative and also contradictory – indication that the authority had a tradition. Enough has been said even in these simple observations to point to a broader conclusion. If we wish to ask why names are included, we have to examine the various writings that contain assigned sayings, looking for the importance accorded to attributions by the authors of the compositions and redactors of the composites of each such compilation. It suffices to note that in the later documents, a variety of positions emerges. One of the most weighty is also most surprising. In the Tosefta, we find that what is attributed in the Mishnah to a given authority will be rewritten, so that the cited sage will say something different from what he is supposed in the Mishnah to have said. Nothing in the Mishnah's statements' theory of matters prepares us for the way in which the Tosefta's authorities treat attributions. So far as they are concerned, I shall now show, while attributions set forth fixed positions on a disputed point, precisely what was subject to dispute was itself a contentious matter.

III. The Uses of Attributions in the Tosefta

Attributions in the Tosefta bear a quite distinct task from those in the Mishnah. A set of names signifies two persistent positions, principles guiding the solution to any given problem. We find in the Tosefta two or more positions assigned to the same named authority, and these positions contradict one another. It follows that attributions bear a quite distinct sense. What they stand for, as we shall see now, is a fixed difference. Party A and Party B will differ in the same way on a variety of issues, and if we know the issues, we also know the positions to be taken by the two parties. Then all consideration of tradition is set aside; all we have in the attribution is the signification of a fixed difference, a predictable position on an unpredictable agenda of issues. A fair analogy, I think, will be the fixed difference between political conservatives and political liberals; whatever the issue, the positions are predictable. Then in place of the House of Shammai and the House of Hillel, X and Y or black and white or pigeon and turtledove would serve equally well. Neither history, nor tradition, nor designation of the accepted and the schismatic position, comes into play, when all that is at stake is the matter of invoking fixed and conventional positions. Then the attributive serves as a formal protocol, nothing more.

What we shall see in the following is that the Mishnah presents a picture of a dispute and the opinions of cited authorities, and the Tosefta provides a quite different account of what was said. The Tosefta has opinions attributed to Judah and Yosé and "others say," and at stake is three distinct positions on the law. So the framers of the Tosefta's composition exhibit access to no single tradition at all; and subject to dispute is not the outcome of a case, but the formulation of the case itself.

Besah Chapter One

A.   The House of Shammai say, "They do not bring dough-offering and priestly gifts to the priest on the festival day,

B.   "whether they were raised up the preceding day or on that same day."

C.   And the House of Hillel permit.

D.   The House of Shammai said to them, "It is an argument by way of analogy.

E.   "The dough-offering and the priestly gifts [Deut. 18:3] are a gift to the priest, and heave-offering is a gift to the priest.

F.   "Just as [on the festival day] they do not bring heave-offering [to a priest], so they do not bring these other gifts [to a priest]."

G.   Said to them the House of Hillel, "No. If you have stated that rule in the case of heave-offering, which one [on the festival] may not designate to begin with, will you apply that same rule concerning the priestly gifts, which [on the festival] one may designate to begin with?"

M. 1:6

The Hillelites allow designating and delivering the priestly gifts owing to the priests from animals slaughtered on the festival day. The House of Shammai do not allow doing so, since the restrictions of the festival day come to bear. We shall now see a completely different picture of matters; I underline the points at which the dispute is reformulated:

A.   Said R. Judah, "The House of Shammai and the House of Hillel concur that they bring [to the priest] gifts <u>which were taken up on the day before the festival along with gifts which were taken on the festival</u> [vs. M. 1:5A-C].

B.   "Concerning what did they differ?

C.   "Concerning [bringing to the priest on the festival] gifts <u>which were taken up on the day before the festival by themselves</u>.

D.   "For the House of Shammai prohibit.

E.   "And the House of Hillel permit.

F.   *"The House of Shammai said, 'It is an argument by way of analogy. The dough-offering and the priestly gifts are a gift to the priest, and heave-offering is a gift to the priest. Just as they do not bring heave-offering [to a priest on the festival day], so they do not bring these other gifts [to a priest on the festival day]'* [M. 1:6D-F].

G.   *"Said to them the House of Hillel, 'No. If you have said that rule in the case of heave-offering, which one may not designate to begin with, will you say that same rule concerning the priestly gifts, which one may designate to begin with?'"* [M. 1:6G].

H.   R. Yosé says, "The House of Shammai and the House of Hillel concur <u>that they do bring the priestly gifts to the priest on the festival day.</u>

I.   "Concerning what do they differ?

J.   <u>"Concerning heave-offering.</u>

K.   "For the House of Shammai prohibit [bringing heave-offering to the priest on the festival day].

L.   "And the House of Hillel permit."

T. 1:12, ed. Lieberman, p. 283,
lines 46-54

A.   *"Said the House of Hillel, 'It is an argument by way of analogy. Dough-offering and priestly gifts are a gift to the priest, and heave-offering is a gift to the priest.* Just as they do bring the priestly gifts to the priest on the festival day, so they should bring heave-offering to the priest on the festival day.'

B.   "Said the House of Shammai to them, 'No. If you have stated the rule in the case of the priestly gifts, which is permitted to be designated [on the festival], will you state that rule concerning heave-offering, which may not be designated [on the festival day]?'"

C.   Others say, "The House of Shammai and the House of Hillel concur <u>that they do not bring heave-offering on a festival.</u>

D.   "Concerning what did they differ?

E.   <u>"Concerning priestly gifts.</u>

F.   "For the House of Shammai prohibit [bringing them to the priest on the festival].

G.   "And the House of Hillel permit" [= M. 1:6A-C]

T. 1:13, ed. Lieberman, pp. 283-
284, lines 54-60

What we see is three distinct positions on what is at stake in the dispute of the Houses of Shammai and Hillel, and, a bit of study would show us, these positions express three distinct principles concerning what is at stake. The second-century authorities are alleged to have three distinct "traditions" on what is at issue between the Houses; each then assigns to the Houses the same language in the same words, along with the same secondary arguments for its distinctive viewpoint. All that varies is the definition of that about which the Houses, to begin with, are conducting their dispute – no small thing!

Now that we have seen ample evidence that attributions serve, even in the Mishnah and the Tosefta, to carry out three quite distinct functions – distinguishing regnant from schismatic opinion, identifying the traditionality of a saying, and marking off fixed points of difference concerning a variable agendum of issues – a measure of humility guides us as we revert to our original question, "Why is the rabbinic literature so interested in coupling utterances and decisions with names?" The question has received only a preliminary answer, but the method before us is clear: we have to ask, document by document, what function is served by attributions, what importance is assigned to them, what difference the presence of an attribution makes in one context or another, and, finally, what conclusions, if any, are drawn from attributions.

IV. Attributed Sayings in the Talmud of the Land of Israel: A Brief Notice

Certainly a survey of the two Talmuds, with their intense interest in the consistency of positions assigned to principal authorities, alongside their quite facile practice of following the dictates of logic, not tradition at all, in switching about among various names the opinions assigned to one or another of them, will yield puzzling evidence. But the outlines of the answer are clear. We may reject as simply irrelevant to the character of the evidence any interest in preserving historical information concerning named figures, for example, for the purpose of biography. The sages of rabbinic documents have opinions, but no biography; many individuals play critical roles in the formation of the several documentary statements, but no individual is accorded a fully articulated individuality, either as to his life, or as to his philosophy or theology.

What conclusions may we draw from this inquiry into the uses of attributions in the earliest of the rabbinic compilations? Let us note, first, what we do not have. For the entire cadre of sages, we have not got a single biography devoted to an individual, or even the raw materials for a sustained and systematic biography; We do not possess a single document produced by a clearly identifiable individual author, a single coherent composite of any consequence at all that concerns itself with a named figure. The counterpart writings for Christianity, the Gospels, the letters of Paul, not to mention the huge collections of signed, personal, individual writings of Church fathers, show us the documents we do not have in rabbinic literature. The theory of authorship, of course, accounts for that fact. A document to warrant recognition – thus to be accorded authority, to be written and copied, or memorized and handed on as tradition – had to attain the approval of the sages' consensus.

That meant that every document in rabbinic literature emerged anonymously, under public sponsorship and authorship, stripped of all marks of individual, therefore idiosyncratic, origin. Personality and individuality stood for schism, and rabbinic literature in its very definition and character aims at the opposite, forming as it does the functional counterpart to the creeds and decisions of Church councils. Framed in mythic terms, the literature aimed to make this theological statement: sages stood in a chain of tradition from Sinai, and the price of inclusion was the acceptance of the discipline of tradition – anonymity, reasoned argument to attain for a private view the public status of a consensus statement. The very definition of tradition that comes to expression in the character of rabbinic literature – God's revelation to Moses at Sinai received and handed on unimpaired and intact in a reliable process of instruction by masters to disciples – accounts for the public, anonymous character of rabbinic writing.

Not a line in the entire rabbinic literature even suggests that schismatic writing existed, even though named statements of individual authorities are preserved on every page of that literature. The point that is proven is simple. People disagreed within a permitted agendum, and the protocol of disagreement always began with the premise of concurrence on all that counted. That was, as we saw, the very goal of rabbinic dialectics: the rationality of dispute, the cogency of theology and of law as a whole. As every named saying we have examined has already shown us, dissenting views, too, found their properly labeled position in rabbinic literature, preserved in the name of the private person who registered dissent in accord with the rules governing the iron consensus of the collegium as a whole.

The final question raised by the ubiquity of attributions to named authorities is, what then is the standing of the named sage? We have seen that the sage is subordinate to tradition, on the one side, and the consensus of sages, on the other. That means the individual as such bore only instrumental importance; he mattered because, and only when, he served as a good example. Or his value derived from the traditions he had in hand from prior authorities. But that fact accords to the individual very high standing indeed – when the individual exemplifies the Torah, attests to tradition, or through wit and sound reasoning demonstrates the validity of a position and compels the consensus to favor his view. So attributions fulfill contradictory tasks. They both call into question the validity of what is attributed and also validate the sage as exemplar of the Torah. The sage stood at that same level of authority as did the Torah, on the one side, and the Mishnah, on the other. Therefore the failure to compose gospels alongside Midrash compilations and Mishnah exegesis is not to be explained away as a byproduct of the conception of revelation through words but not through persons that is imputed to the Judaism of the Dual Torah. Quite to the contrary, God reveals the Torah not only through words handed down from Sinai in the form of the Torah, written and oral, but also through the lives and deeds of saints, that is, sages. The same modes of exegetical inquiry pertaining to the Mishnah and Scripture apply without variation to statements made by rabbis of the contemporary period themselves.

A single example of the superficially contradictory, but deeply harmonious, meaning imputed to attributions suffices. For that purpose we turn to the way in which the rabbis of the Yerushalmi proposed to resolve differences of opinion. Precisely in the same way in which talmudic rabbis settled disputes in the Mishnah and so attained a consensus about the law of the Mishnah, they handled disputes among themselves. The importance of that fact for our argument again is simple. The rabbis, represented in the Yerushalmi, treated their own contemporaries exactly as they treated the then-ancient authorities of the Mishnah. In their minds the status accorded to the Mishnah, as a derivative of the Torah, applied equally to sages' teachings. In the following instance we see how the same discourse attached to (1) a Mishnah rule is assigned as well to one in (2) the Tosefta and, at the end, to differences among (3) the Yerushalmi's authorities.

Yerushalmi Ketubot 5:1.VI

A. R. Jacob bar Aha, R. Alexa in the name of Hezekiah: "The law accords with the view of R. Eleazar b. Azariah, who stated, **If she was widowed or divorced at the stage of betrothal, the virgin collects only two hundred zuz and the widow, a maneh. If she was widowed or divorced at the stage of a consummated marriage, she collects the full amount [M. Ket. 5:1E,D].**"

B. R. Hananiah said, "The law accords with the view of R. Eleazar b. Azariah."

C. Said Abbayye, "They said to R. Hananiah, 'Go and shout [outside whatever opinion you like.' But] R. Jonah, R. Zeira in the name of R. Jonathan said, 'The law accords with the view of R. Eleazar b. Azariah.' [Yet] R. Yosa bar Zeira in the name of R. Jonathan said, 'The law does not accord with the view of R. Eleazar b. Azariah.' [So we do not in fact know the decision.]"

D. Said R. Yosé, "We had a mnemonic: Hezekiah and R. Jonathan both say one thing."

E. For it has been taught on Tannaite authority:

F. **He whose son went abroad, and whom they told, "Your son has died,"**

G. **and who went and wrote over all his property to someone else as a gift,**

H. **and whom they afterward informed that his son was yet alive –**

I. **his deed of gift remains valid.**

J. **R. Simeon b. Menassia says, "His deed of gift is not valid, for if he had known that his son was alive, he would never have made such a gift" [T. Ket. 4:14E-H].**

K. Now R. Jacob bar Aha [= A] said, "The law is in accord with the view of R. Eleazar b. Azariah, and the opinion of R. Eleazar b. Azariah is the same in essence as that of R. Simeon b. Menassia."

L. Now R. Yannai said to R. Hananiah, "Go and shout [outside whatever you want].

M. "But, said R. Yosé bar Zeira in the name of R. Jonathan, 'The law is not in accord with R. Eleazar b. Azariah.'"

N. But in fact the case was to be decided in accord with the view of R. Eleazar b. Azariah.

What is important here is that the Talmud makes no distinction whatever when deciding the law of disputes (1) in the Mishnah, (2) in the Tosefta, and (3) among talmudic rabbis. The same already formed colloquy applied at the outset to the Mishnah's dispute is then held equally applicable to the Tosefta's. The process of thought is the main thing, without regard to the document to which the process applies. Scripture, the Mishnah, the sage – the three spoke with equal authority. True, one had to come into alignment with the other, the Mishnah with Scripture, the sage with the Mishnah. But it was not the case that one component of the Torah, of God's word to Israel, stood within the sacred circle, another beyond. Interpretation and what was interpreted, exegesis and text, belonged together. The sage, or rabbi, constitutes the third component in a tripartite canon of the Torah, because, while Scripture and the Mishnah govern what the sage knows, in the Yerushalmi as in the Bavli it is the sage who authoritatively speaks about them. What sages were willing to do to the Mishnah in the Yerushalmi and Bavli is precisely what they were prepared to do to Scripture – impose upon it their own judgment of its meaning.

The sage speaks with authority about the Mishnah and the Scripture. As much as those documents of the Torah, the sage, too, therefore has authority deriving from revelation. He himself may participate in the process of revelation. There is no material difference. Since that is so, the sage's book, whether the Yerushalmi or the Bavli to the Mishnah or Midrash to Scripture, belongs to the Torah, that is, is revealed by God. It also forms part of the Torah, a fully canonical document. The reason, then, is that the sage is like Moses, "our rabbi," who received torah and wrote the Torah. So while the canon of the Torah was in three parts, two verbal, one incarnate – Scripture, Mishnah, sage – the sage, in saying what the other parts meant and in embodying that meaning in his life and thought, took primacy of place. If no document organized itself around sayings and stories of sages, it was because that was superfluous. Why so? Because all documents, equally, whether Scripture, whether Mishnah, whether Yerushalmi, gave full and complete expression of deeds and deliberations of sages, beginning, after all, with Moses, our rabbi.

V. Differentiating the Premises as to Attributions and their Meaning Characteristic of Diverse Rabbinic Documents

A few concluding observations suffice to return us to our starting point. No document in rabbinic literature is signed by a named author or is so labeled (except in a few instances long after the fact, for example, Judah the Patriarch wrote the Mishnah) as to represent the opinion of a lone individual. In their intrinsic traits of uniform discourse all documents speak out of the single, undifferentiated voice of Sinai, and each makes a statement of the Torah of Sinai and within that Torah. That anonymity, indicative for theological reasons, comes to expression in the highly formalized rhetoric of the canonical writings, which denies the possibility of the individuation not only of the writings themselves, but also of the sayings attributed to authorities in those writings.

Books such as the Mishnah, Sifré to Deuteronomy, Genesis Rabbah, or the Bavli, that after formulation were accepted as part of the canon of Judaism, that is, of "the one whole Torah of Moses our rabbi revealed by God at Sinai," do not contain answers to questions of definition that commonly receive answers within the pages of a given book. Such authors as (the school of) Matthew or Luke, Josephus, even the writers of Ezra-Nehemiah, would have found such a policy surprising. And while Socrates did not write, Plato and Aristotle did – and they signed their own names (or did the equivalent in context). In antiquity books or other important writings, for example, letters and treatises, ordinarily, though not always, bore the name of the author or at least an attribution, for example, Aristotle's or Paul's name, or the attribution to Enoch or Baruch or Luke. For no document in the canon of Judaism produced in late antiquity, by contrast, is there a named author internal to the document. No document in that canon contains within itself a statement of a clear-cut date of composition, a defined place or circumstance in which a book is written, a sustained and ongoing argument to which we readily gain access, or any of the other usual indicators by which we define the authorship, therefore the context and the circumstance, of a book.

The purpose of the sages who in the aggregate created the canonical writings of the Judaism of the Dual Torah is served by not specifying differentiating traits such as time, place, and identity of the author or the authorship. The Judaic equivalent of the Biblical canon ("the Old Testament and the New Testament") is "the one whole Torah of Moses, our rabbi," and that "one, whole Torah" presents single books as undifferentiated episodes in a timeless, ahistorical setting: Torah revealed to Moses by God at Mount Sinai, but written down long afterward. Received in a canonical process of transmission under the auspices of a religious system, any canonical writing, by definition, enjoys authority and status within that canon and system. Hence it is deemed to speak for a community and to represent, and contribute to, the consensus of that community. Without a named author, a canonical writing may be represented, on the surface, as the statement of a consensus. That consensus derives not from an identifiable writer or even school but from the anonymous authorities behind the document as we have it. A consensus of an entire community, the community of Judaism, reaches its full human realization in the sage. That is why the sage will be mentioned by name – but at the same time represented as exemplary, therefore subordinate; exemplary, not individual; exemplary, not schismatic. In that context writing down of that consensus will not permit individual traits of rhetoric to differentiate writer from writer or writing from writing. The individual obliterates the marks of individuality in serving the holy people by writing a work that will become part of the Torah, and stories about individuals will serve, in that context, only so far as they exemplify and realize traits characteristic of all Torah sages.

Index

South Florida Studies in the History of Judaism

DATE DUE

12/31/13			
			Printed in USA